Improving the Quality of Student Learning

based on the

Improving Student Learning Project
funded by the
Council for National Academic Awards

Graham Gibbs

Technical and Education Services Ltd.

First published 1992
by Technical and Educational Services Ltd.
37 Ravenswood Road, Bristol, BS6 6BW

©1992 Oxford Centre for Staff Development

Typeset by Avril Smith
Cover design by Jason Mortimer
Printed by Billings Ltd., Worcester

ISBN 0 947885 80 3

Available from:
Plymbridge Distributors, Estover, Plymouth, PL6 7PZ. Tel. 0752 695745, Fax. 0752 777603

To Vicky

Contents

About the Author

Graham Gibbs is Head of the Oxford Centre for Staff Development, the largest staff development agency in higher education in the UK. He was previously Head of the Educational Methods Unit at Oxford Polytechnic and Head of the Study Methods Research Group at the Open University. He has managed national research and development projects such as the 'Teaching More Students' project for the PCFC, and has written widely about student learning and about teaching methods in higher education.

Acknowledgements

The initial idea and funding for the 'Improving Student Learning' project came from the CNAA and without their support this book would not have been written. I would particularly like to thank Nigel Nixon for his help throughout and his trust that everything would work out.

The heart of this book is the case studies. I would like to acknowledge the commitment, and professionalism as teachers, of the innovators responsible for them, many of whom have become friends: Julie Hartley, Sandra Watson and Iain Marshall, Alan Jenkins, Peter Griffiths and Brian Lowe, Alan Davies and Barry Jackson, David Lane and Angela Brew, Geoffrey Millward, Kay Stachura, Brian Mitchell and Ewan Knox. If the rest of the lecturers in higher education were like them what an exciting place it would be!

Finally I'd like to thank Felix Lam for administering the whole project so smoothly. As usual I wouldn't have managed without her.

Preface

This book is one outcome of the 'Improving Student Learning' project undertaken by the Oxford Centre for Staff Development and funded by the Council for National Academic Awards. The funding provided support for eight courses to undertake detailed case studies as they introduced innovations designed to improve the quality of student learning. The other outcomes of the project included two national conferences and a poster-sized leaflet describing the project which was distributed to 30,000 lecturers in Polytechnics and Colleges in the UK in 1992.

Before this book had been published, and before the leaflet had been distributed, there had already been an extraordinary level of interest in the project. Over 500 lecturers had requested to receive Newsletters about the development of the project and over 1,000 had requested a copy of a paper outlining its conceptual framework. Institutions had copied this paper for distribution to every member of their staff. Workshops and conference presentations had been requested in over 20 institutions.

The project also engendered a sense of achievement and loyalty from the innovators involved: those who undertook the case studies. For them, and for me, it was a rare opportunity to monitor a course properly and to discuss the changes and the consequences for student learning with other lecturers who also cared about quality.

The project took place at a time when student numbers in higher education were increasing rapidly without adequate funding, and when most people in higher education saw a depressing decline in the quality of students' learning experience. The contexts within which much of the innovation reported here took were sometimes disheartening. The success of many of the innovations was inspiring. It showed that with care and understanding, demonstrable improvements in quality were possible even in unpromising surroundings.

Some of the innovations were so successful that their contexts started changing immediately—other staff got involved, the ideas spread quickly and the methods were adopted readily. In other contexts the innovations are vulnerable. The lack of support for the innovators, resource pressures and conservative students could all pose threats. Innovators are in a risky business.

The case studies reported here show what is possible and how to demonstrate that it is possible. I hope this book provides support for innovators everywhere who need arguments to support their experience, evidence to back their arguments, and belief to carry them through the opposition and practical problems they will encounter. In higher education today anyone who cares about quality needs all the support they can find.

Chapter 1

The nature of quality in learning

If we are concerned with improving the quality of student learning then it is important to have a definition of what quality in learning consists of. The CNAA, who sponsored the 'Improving Student Learning' project have their own definition in their formal description of the general aims of a programme of study in higher education:

> '... the development of students' intellectual and imaginative powers; their understanding and judgement; their problem-solving skills; their ability to communicate; their ability to see relationships within what they have learned and to perceive their field of study in a broader perspective. The programme must aim to stimulate an enquiring, analytical and creative approach, encouraging independent judgement and critical self-awareness.'

This definition of quality has had less impact on the quality of learning, despite two decades of CNAA validation of courses in Polytechnics and Colleges, than might have been hoped. It is clear that not all courses achieve these goals for all students. The HMI commentary 'The English Polytechnics' (1989) reported:

- an over-dependence on one way of teaching and learning—often the formal lecture—so that students do not develop a range of skills appropriate to higher education;

- spoon feeding in lectures, seminars and practical work, so that students become over-dependent on the information selected and provided for them by their teachers;

- assessment methods which place too high a premium on the ability to recall factual information.

1

The HMI report identified both a key feature of quality in student learning—the difference between attempting to memorise the subject matter and attempting to understand and to apply knowledge—and the role of teaching and assessment methods in influencing the quality of student learning. This fundamental difference in the quality of student learning, and the influence of courses upon it, has been explored extensively in research into student learning. What follows is an account of some of that literature which provides the conceptual framework for the case studies in Chapters 4—13.

Surface and deep approaches to learning

When students go about learning tasks they vary in their approach. Every lecturer has experienced students who seem determined to give back, in essays and reports, exactly what they were given, in lectures. Other students strive to develop their own perspectives and syntheses of the subject. This may sometimes involve a difference in ability, but most often it involves a difference in intention: students are trying to achieve different things. These two extreme intentions have been termed a surface approach and a deep approach. Through extensive interview studies (Marton and Säljö, 1976, Marton and Säljö, 1984) the following definitions have been generated, illustrated here with quotes from students.

Surface approach

The student reduces what is to be learnt to the status of unconnected facts to be memorised. The learning task is to reproduce the subject matter at a later date (eg in an exam).

> 'It would have been more interesting if I'd known that I wasn't going to be tested on it afterwards, 'cos in that case I'd've more, you know, thought about what it said instead of all the time trying to think : "Now I must remember this and now I must remember that".'

Deep approach

The student attempts to make sense of what is to be learnt, which consists of ideas and concepts. This involves thinking, seeking integration between components and between tasks, and 'playing' with ideas.

> 'I tried to look for ... you know, the principal ideas ... I tried to think what it was all about ... I though about how he had built up the whole thing.'

An approach is not the same thing as a skill. It is primarily about the learner's intention. It can be difficult to identify students' approach just by looking at their lecture notes, for example. You might need to ask the students what they were trying to do when they were taking the notes, and what they were thinking about.

2

Surface approaches are very common

It has been argued that while a surface approach may be common in schools, or perhaps in poor students in the first year in higher education, it is not really an issue beyond that. It is assumed to be a problem which automatically goes away with maturity and experience. This is not the case. Evidence of the prevalence of a surface approach is deeply disturbing. In the UK a surface approach is common in all subject areas, and more common in Universities than in Polytechnics (Ramsden, 1983). In higher education in Australia, students have been found to adopt a deep approach to a lesser extent as they progress through their courses. This phenomenon is more marked in Colleges of Advanced Education than in Universities, more common in science than in arts, and more common in undergraduates who do not intend to continue on to postgraduate studies than in those who do (*cf* Biggs, 1982). A deep approach also declines throughout high school in Australia, with Form 5 pupils adopting a deep approach to a lesser extent than Form 2 pupils.

A surface approach is disastrous

The first year of undergraduate courses in physics and chemistry commonly repeats much of the 'A-level' syllabuses because although students who have got good 'A-level' grades can substitute numbers in formulae, follow algorithms for solving standard problems and remember the definitions of terms, they do not adequately understand the concepts involved. When the quality of learning outcomes are examined through interviews this frequently reveals a very different picture than that revealed by exams where students can accumulate marks for memorisation. There is now a considerable body of evidence of the lack of understanding of key concepts of students who have successfully passed courses, in a variety of subjects and at a variety of levels. For example a study of a first year undergraduate economics course found that few students had understood a range of key economics concepts. Indeed the quality of understanding of several concepts was actually poorer at the end of the course than before the course started. Results on a conventional exam revealed none of this failure (Dahlgren, 1984).

As ways have been developed of identifying the quality of students' understanding, so it has been possible to study, under controlled conditions, the impact of a deep or a surface approach on the quality of learning outcomes. It has become abundantly clear that it is very unlikely that a student who takes a surface approach will gain a full understanding of a concept, an overview of a topic, a grasp the main ideas in a chapter, be able to distinguish principles from examples, write an essay with a logical argument, or recognise the key ideas in a lecture. Essays, or summaries of chapters, written by students who have taken a surface approach, are quite different in structure to those of students who have taken a deep approach. A surface approach produces a 'multistructural' essay (containing a list of unrelated items) while a deep approach usually produces a 'relational' answer (integrating items into a structure) or an 'extended abstract' answer (which goes beyond the immediate topic and applies ideas to a related issue or area). Biggs, (1990) summarised the literature in the following way:

> 'Relationships between such approaches and outcome are exceptionally
> strong: studies ... show that a surface approach, almost without excep-
> tion, leads to a quantitative outcome of unstructured detail, and a deep
> approach to an appropriately structured outcome.'

It may be argued that full understanding is not always required, and that an ability
to memorise without understanding is sometimes enough. Studies have shown that
a surface approach does tend to produce marginally higher scores on tests of factual
recall immediately after studying. However this small advantage is quickly lost. A
surface approach leads to rapid forgetting and as little as a week later students who
have taken a deep approach will score far higher than those who took a surface
approach, even on tests of factual recall (Marton and Wenestam, 1978).

Evidence on long-term retention of knowledge from undergraduate courses supports these findings. For example in a study of what cognitive psychology students
remembered after they had taken a course, low-level knowledge, concerned with facts,
names and the names of concepts, showed rapid forgetting. In contrast knowledge
which involved understanding showed little forgetting even over 11 years. Further,
while coursework grades were a very good predictor of long term recall, exam results
did not predict long term recall at all. Students who did well in the exam subsequently remembered no more than students who did poorly. This can be interpreted
as being due to the kinds of learning characteristic of intensive revision for exams
involving a surface approach. In contrast to the kinds of learning involved in independent experimental and practical work which in the course being studied were
required for assessed coursework led to good long term recall. (Cohen et al 1992).
Even where memory is valued a surface approach is very ineffective except in the
very short term.

A surface approach is also not successful on whole courses. Both interview and
questionnaire studies have shown students who take a surface approach to gain lower
marks and poorer degree results and to be more likely to fail (*cf* Svensson, 1977).
The effects are often quite dramatic. Given the very limited effects of students'
'A-level' scores, intelligence and study skills on their performance in higher education, evidence of the impact the impact of the approach students take is especially
impressive.

These studies have spanned subject areas as diverse as humanities, science, computing and social science, in four different countries, using different research methods. They have spanned small specialist courses and large undergraduate degree
programmes containing over 40 disciplines and over 2,000 students. The range and
diversity of these studies leaves no doubt that a surface approach has a disastrous
impact on the quality of learning outcomes.

Most students can adopt both surface and deep approaches to their learning

The approach a student takes to a learning task is not fixed: it is not like a personality characteristic or intelligence. Students often take a consistent approach in their everyday studies and take the same approach in experimental studies. However such evidence hides as much as it reveals. Science students have been found to vary both between learning tasks, depending on the nature of the task, and within tasks, depending on the demands of parts of problems, for example (Laurillard, 1979). And the majority of students both understand the difference between a surface and a deep approach and describe themselves as adopting whichever of the approaches seems appropriate. A small proportion of students, however, describe themselves as always taking a surface approach, and have difficulty understanding what the deep/surface distinction means. These students adopt a surface approach because they have a conception of learning which does not make it possible for them to go about learning in any other way .

Students develop an increasingly sophisticated conception of learning

Underlying the approach students take is their understanding of what learning itself consists of. This understanding changes, influenced by the context students find themselves in and by the learning demands these contexts make. Studies have identified five stages in the development of students' understanding, listed here with examples of the kinds of things students who have these conceptions say.

1. Learning as an increase in knowledge. The student will often see learning as something done to them by teachers rather than as something they do to, or for, themselves.

   'To gain some knowledge is learning ... We obviously want to learn more. I want to know as much as possible'.

2. Learning as memorising. The student has an active role in memorising, but the information being memorised is not transformed in any way.

   'Learning is about getting it into your head. You've just got to keep writing it out and eventually it will go in.'

3. Learning as acquiring facts or procedures which are to be used. What you learn is seen to include skills, algorithms, formulae which you apply etc which you will need in order to do things at a later date, but there is still no transformation of what is learnt by the learner.

   'Well it's about learning the thing so you can do it again when you are asked to, like in an exam.'

4. Learning as making sense. The student makes active attempts to abstract meaning in the process of learning. This may only involve academic tasks.

> 'Learning is about trying to understand things so you can see what is going on. You've got to be able to explain things, not just remember them.'

5. Learning as understanding reality. Learning enables you to perceive the world differently. This has also been termed 'personally meaningful learning'.

> 'When you have really learnt something you kind of see things you couldn't see before. Everything changes.'

There are other developmental schemes, describing how students change in the sophistication of their perception of the learning tasks they face, which embody very similar descriptions (*cf* Perry, 1970).

Stages 4 and 5 are clearly qualitatively different from stages 1—3. Students who understand what learning is at levels 1, 2 or 3 have trouble comprehending what a deep approach consists of and are very unlikely to take a deep approach to learning tasks. Students who are at levels 4 or 5 can take either a deep or a surface approach, depending on the task and their perception of its demands. The connection between these underlying conceptions of learning and the approach students take to specific learning tasks is so strong that it is possible to predict the quality of learning outcomes directly from students' conceptions of learning. All you need to know about a student is that she has a conception of learning at level 1, 2 or 3 and you can be fairly certain that she will only derive a superficial and fragmentary understanding from, for example, reading a chapter (Van Rossum and Schenk, 1984).

For some students, then, their limited understanding of what learning consists of prevents them from approaching learning tasks in a deep way and therefore from learning effectively. Two important questions about such crude and disabling conceptions of learning are: 'where do they come from?' and 'can they be changed?'.

As well as being asked about what they think learning is, students have been asked what they think good teaching consists of (Van Rossum and Taylor, 1987). Some think that the teacher should do all the work and make all the decisions. The teacher should select the subject matter, present it in teacher-controlled classes, devise tests and mark students on how well they have learnt the material which has been presented. What is to be learnt and what learning outcomes should look like is completely defined by the teacher (a 'closed' conception of teaching). Others think that while the teacher has responsibility for setting the learning climate, for making learning resources available, and for supporting students, all the responsibility lies with the student: responsibility for selecting learning goals, devising appropriate learning activities and for judging when learning outcomes are satisfactory (an 'open' conception of teaching). The 'closed', conception of teaching is held almost exclusively by students with conceptions of learning at levels 1, 2 or 3, while the latter, 'open', conception of teaching is held by students with conceptions of learning at levels 4 or 5. This relationship is summarised in the table below.

Conception of learning	Conception of teaching
Reproducing (levels 1, 2 and 3)	**Closed** Teacher selects content, presents it and tests whether it has 'stuck'
Making sense (levels 4 and 5)	**Open** Learner functions independently with the facilitation of the teacher

There is also evidence from questionnaire studies that students who take a surface approach have a different view of what good teaching consists of from that of stduents who take a deep approach (Entwistle and Tait, 1990).The key issue here is whether students see good teaching as 'closed' teaching because they have a reproductive conception of learning, or whether they have a reproductive conception of learning because they have been experiencing 'closed' teaching. I believe the latter explanation, for three reasons. First, it is easy to see even young children taking a deep approach to learning. They are able to tell you when they don't understand and they can sometimes surprise you by announcing when they have 'really understood' something which previously they had only learnt by rote (cf Rogers 1969). It seems as though an implicit understanding of different levels of learning is somehow lost, through schooling. Second, High School pupils have been found to progressively abandon a deep approach over the four years of their studies, implying an effect on their studying of the type of teaching commonly used to prepare pupils for that level of exams. Third, longitudinal studies of students in higher education have plotted rapid developments in the sophistication of students' conceptions of learning, attributed directly to the nature of learning tasks and assessment the students have experienced (cf Gibbs et al 1984). It seems that students can become more sophisticated as learners as a consequence of their experience of more open-ended learning environments. This is a well documented and commonplace experience of students undertaking third year undergraduate project and dissertation work after two years of lecture-based and examined courses.

This is beginning to answer the second question raised above: 'can students' conceptions of learning be changed?'. It seems that the experience of learning tasks which make more sophisticated demands on students can be an effective way to develop students as learners. Study skills courses which focus on techniques such as reading, note-taking and time management (ie skills which can be used to implement either a surface or a deep approach) are largely ineffective. One study found that the

7

only discernible outcome of such a study skills course was an increase in the extent to which students adopted a surface approach (Ramsden et al 1986). Direct attempts to develop students' conceptions of learning outside the context of courses need to focus on the purpose of learning tasks, and on students' awareness of what they are doing, rather than on techniques.

Inappropriate course design, teaching methods and assessment can foster a surface approach

The following passages are extracts from interviews conducted at a Polytechnic as part of a survey of students' approaches to studying. The first illustrates a deep approach being taken in the context of a geography course. The interviewer was enquiring about what the student was doing whilst reading for an essay involving some quotations provided by his lecturer.

> Interviewer: 'When you are going through and underlining, what sort of things are going through your mind?'
> Student: 'Well, I read it, I read it very slowly, trying to concentrate on what it means, what the actual passage means. Obviously I've read the quotations a few times and I've got it in my mind, what they mean. I really try to read it slowly. There is a lot of meaning behind it. You have to really kind of get into it and take every passage, every sentence, and try to really think "Well what does this mean?" You mustn't regurgitate what David is saying because that's not the idea of the exercise, so I suppose it's really original ideas in this one, kind of getting it all together.'

This contrasts starkly with this second extract, of a student describing taking a surface approach on a computing course. The student had just described taking notes in lectures whilst thinking about something other than the lecture content, in order not to interfere with the mechanics of getting the notes down, and had described what learning had involved on the course.

> Interviewer: 'When you use the word learning in relation to this course, what do you mean?'
> Student: 'Getting enough facts so that you can write something relevant in the exam. You've got enough information so you can write an essay on it. What I normally do is learn certain headings. I'll write a question down, about four, five different headings, which in an exam I can go: "Introduction" and I'll look at the next heading and I know what I've got to write about without really thinking about it really. I know the facts about it. I go to the next heading and regurgitate.'

These quotes may at first seem no different to many others which have been documented about the stark and depressing difference between students' approaches to studying. However there are two additional features of these quotes which make them special. First, the student in the second extract obtained an upper second class honours degree. It is clearly possible to achieve a good degree whilst only memorising if the assessment system works in the way the student describes. Second, these two extracts do not illustrate two different students but involve the same student on two different courses. This is not a lazy, stupid, incompetent or unaware student. He has simply responded strategically to the perceived demands of the two different courses. What matters here is what it is about courses which can lead competent students to take such an extreme surface approach, with all the negative consequences this has for learning.

Many studies have looked at the relationship between the approach students take to their courses and a number of features of the courses in order to identify what it is about courses which affects students. Studies have involved laboratory 'experiments', the use of questionnaires and the use of depth interviews, in Sweden, the UK and Australia. Some of the studies have been very large, involving thousands of students and scores of academic departments across a wide range of subject areas and institutions (*cf* Biggs, 1989a, Crooks, 1988, Ramsden 1987). The table below summarises the findings of these studies.

Course characteristics associated with a surface approach

- A heavy workload

- Relatively high class contact hours

- An excessive amount of course material

- A lack of opportunity to pursue subjects in depth

- A lack of choice over subjects and a lack of choice over the method of study

- A threatening and anxiety provoking assessment system

The Course Perceptions Questionnaire (Entwistle and Ramsden, 1983) was developed to identify aspects of course which related to the approaches to learning students took on the courses. Developed further into the Course Experience Questionnaire (Ramsden, 1991) it has been demonstrated, in national scale studies, to distinguish reliably between the quality of whole degree programmes and is being used as a performance indicator.

It is important to recognise that a surface approach is not necessarily a consequence of these course characteristics, and that students' perceptions of course characteristics may differ from those of teachers. Both continuous assessment and final exams, for example, can be experienced as anxiety provoking by students. It

9

is likely to be contextual factors which determine the extent to which these course characteristics have negative consequences.

There is a considerable amount of evidence that assessment systems dominate what students are oriented towards in their learning. Even where lecturers say that they want students to be creative and thoughtful, students often recognise that what is really necessary, or at least what is sufficient, is to memorise. The following psychology student illustrates this:

> 'I hate to say it but what you have got to do is to bung down a list of 'facts'; you write down the important points and memorize those, then you'll do all right in the exam ... if you can give a bit of factual information—so and so did that, and concluded that—for two sides of writing, then you'll get a good mark.' (Ramsden, 1984, p144)

Even where lecturers really do want students to take a deep approach, the assessment system often allows students to get by despite taking a surface approach. In the case of the Geography student quoted above, taking a surface approach was quite successful in terms of marks on his Computing course.

Of course sometimes students misread the requirements of the assessment system and select a surface approach by mistake. This is often because it isn't clear enough what the real demands are. In experimental studies which lack the context of a real course to help students to guess what they are supposed to be doing when they are learning, there is very strong tendency for students to adopt a surface approach. If students are uncertain what is required then they tend to take a surface approach.

Appropriate course design, teaching methods and assessment can foster a deep approach

Avoiding a surface approach is one thing, but what encourages a deep approach? Studies have identified a number of factors which are, in effect, the obverse of factors which foster a surface approach: relatively low class contact hours, intrinsic interest in the subject and freedom in learning. Freedom may involve choice over content or method of learning or scope for intellectual independence. An additional factor is 'perceived good teaching'. What 'good teaching' consists of has been identified through many studies of teaching processes which are associated with a deep approach. Four key elements have been identified by Biggs (1989b):

1. **Motivational context** Deep learning is more likely when students' motivation is intrinsic and when the student experiences a need to know something. Adults learn best what they need to learn in order to carry out tasks which matter to them. Students are likely to need to be involved in selecting what is to be learnt and in planning how the learning should take place if they are to experience 'ownership' of it. The motivational context is established by the emotional climate of the learning. While a positive emotional and motivational climate may be a necessary condition for deep learning, anxiety and instrumentalism may be sufficient conditions for surface learning.

2. Learner activity

Students need to be active rather than passive. Deep learning is associated with doing. If the learner is actively involved, then more connections will be made both with past learning and between new concepts. Doing is not sufficient for learning, however. Learning activity must be planned, reflected upon and processed, and related to abstract conceptions.

3. Interaction with others

It is often easier to negotiate meaning and to manipulate ideas with others than alone. The importance of discussion for learning is not a new idea, though there is precious little discussion in much of higher education. Interaction can take many forms other than conventional tutorials and seminars, and autonomous student groups and peer tutoring can be very effective. Studies have even shown the student who does the tutoring to learn more than the student who is tutored, confirming the everyday experience that the best way to learn something is to teach it.

4. A well structured knowledge base

Without existing concepts it is impossible to make sense of new concepts. It is vital that students' existing knowledge and experience are brought to bear in learning. The subject matter being learnt must also be well structured and integrated. The structure of knowledge is more visible to and and more useful to students where it is clearly displayed, where content is taught in integrated wholes rather than in small separate pieces, and where knowledge is required to be related to other knowledge rather than learned in isolation. Interdisciplinary approaches also contribute to a well structured knowledge base.

The extent to which course design, teaching and assessment methods embody these four elements will determine whether they are likely to foster a deep approach. Problem-based learning, for example, embodies all four of these elements. Marked differences have been found in the extent of deep approaches to learning in a traditional medical school compared with a medical school using problem-based learning. (Newble and Clarke, 1986). The next chapter examines methods and strategies which embody these elements in a variety of ways.

Chapter 2

Strategies for fostering a deep approach

This chapter outlines nine strategies for improving the quality of student learning by fostering a deep approach. These strategies overlap in several respects and many innovations embody features from several of the strategies. The important features of these strategies are the extent to which they embody the four key elements introduced in Chapter 1: a motivational context, learner activity, interactions with others and a well structured knowledge base.

Strategy 1: Independent learning

Independent learning involves giving students greater autonomy and control over choice of subject matter, learning methods, pace of study and assessment of learning outcomes. For example the Suffolk College offers a DipHE by independent study based on that developed at the Polytechnic of East London. There is no fixed syllabus and very few boundaries as to what would be considered an acceptable course of study. Instead students negotiate a learning contract. This involves students reviewing their existing knowledge and setting personal goals, planning how to achieve these goals and then using the contract as a basis of assessment as to whether these goals have been achieved. Over 2,500 students have achieved DipHEs at the Polytechnic of East London in this way (see Percy and Ramsden, 1980).

The DipHE by independent study involves all four key elements which foster a deep approach: a sound basis in existing knowledge, high student motivation through selection of personally relevant learning goals, learning activities, selected by students, and interaction with others through the use of 'specialist groups' and workshops. However it is the motivational context which is its strength. Student feel a great deal of commitment to and 'ownership' of their learning when negotiated in this way.

Most innovations involving independent learning are less extensive and less open-ended than this example and tends to follow periods of more conventional study which is designed to provide the knowledge base. It may involve negotiation of only one aspect of the curriculum—for example which topics a seminar series covers. Project work, described below, can be seen as independent learning involving less independence. Chapter 5 describes the use of negotiated learning contracts for work-based learning.

Methods associated with this strategy include the use of learning contracts (Knowles, 1986), self and peer assessment, project work, and the negotiation of goals, learning methods, assignments, and assessment methods, assessment criteria and marks.

Strategy 2: Personal development

This strategy emphasises motivational context, especially personal involvement in learning. Typically there is a focus on the engagement of the whole person, feelings as well as intellect, in the learning process. (Rogers, 1969). The role of the lecturer is quite different to that in conventional teaching and involves three main features.

- Creating a learning climate which is safe and supportive, within which learners feel able to take risks in their learning, challenging existing assumptions and going beyond past learning.

- Facilitating learners in taking responsibility for their learning. The development of student autonomy may be a primary educational goal.

- An emphasis on the expression of feelings and on learning to have more open access to one's own feelings and more sensitive response to the feelings of others. The integration of the affect and the intellect is also a primary educational goal.

The method most commonly associated with this strategy is group work which allows discussion of group process and individual feelings as well as of the content of learning. However methods are not seen as important compared with the underlying rationale and the facilitative style of the lecturer. The case study in Chapter 11 involves, amongst other innovations, a focus on personal development as part of the education of physiotherapists who needed to explore their personal reactions to different client groups.

Strategy 3: Problem-based learning

Problem-based learning involves learning through tackling relevant problems. This is distinct from learning how to solve problems (problem-solving). In problem-based learning the problem may not be solvable, but nevertheless provides a rich environment for learning. The aim is to learn rather than to solve the problem. Problem-based learning is also distinct from applying knowledge to problems (project work). In problem-based learning there is no prior presentation of subject matter. (Boud and Felletti, 1991). Students discover what they need to learn about through being confronted with problems, and then learn what they need to in order to be able to tackle the problem. In some applications of this method there is no emphasis on actually 'solving' the problem. Problems are simply exploited for their learning potential, after which students move on to the next problem. The main features of the strategy are:

- Relevant problems. Problem-based learning is most common in professional courses such as medicine and engineering where students are given real-world problems of the kind a professional would be faced with. In well-developed applications the problems are carefully designed to involve all the important parts of the syllabus. Students may select and negotiate their way through problems in order to make sure that they 'cover' the syllabus.

- A 'need to know'. What students go off and learn about is determined by what is necessary to tackle the problem. This generates a great deal of highly focussed motivation.

- Integration of knowledge. Real-world problems are very often large scale and interdisciplinary. Students do not experience knowledge in artificially discrete packages.

- Interaction. Problem-based learning almost always employs groups of students working co-operatively, sharing ideas, dividing up the learning to be done, briefing each other and solving problems co-operatively.

Problem-based learning therefore involves all four elements which foster a deep approach. Chapter 7 describes a problem-based engineering course.

Strategy 4: Reflection

Students who take a surface approach can be unaware of how and what they are learning, and unaware of the real demands of their courses. Reflection on learning, both on process and content, can help students to take charge of their learning even in highly constraining circumstances, and to move towards a deep approach Boud et al, 1985). Reflection can be particularly important in the context of professional and sandwich courses involving work placement, where reflection can help to turn experience into learning. Reflection emphasises two of the four elements: learner activity, in that it involves learners in actively processing their learning, and a well structured knowledge base, through making students' own knowledge, and gaps in their knowledge, more apparent to them.

Methods which encourage reflection include the use of learning diaries, reflective journals and portfolios of work, discussion of learning strategies, specially designed reflective exercises run by lecturers, and the use of video, audio and observers in the context of learning which involves performance or behavioural skills.

Chapter 7 describes the use of reflective journals and learning logs in Engineering and Chapter 12 describes the use of learning logs in Law. Reflection on learning is a also a theme of several of the other case studies.

Strategy 5: Independent group work

This strategy focuses mainly on the element of interaction. Interaction between students is also inherently motivating and encourages a range of learning activity.

Methods which emphasise independent group work include group-based project work and peer tutoring, in which students teach each other. Independent group work often takes place within other strategies (eg problem-based learning) and is also used as a fine-tuning methods within conventional courses (eg the use of student-led seminar groups).

Interaction in class is a feature of Chapters 6, 9 and 13. Interaction in independent groups is a feature of Chapters 4, 7,8, 10 and 12.

Strategy 6: Learning by doing

Experiential learning emphasises the element of learner activity. Methods associated with experiential learning are enormously diverse (Gibbs, 1988) and are common to several of the strategies listed here, especially independent learning, problem-centred learning and reflection. In this project their is a focus on the deliberate introduction into courses of the concrete experience of real-world tasks as way of encouraging students to become:

- more involved, so increasing motivation;

- more active;

- more aware of their existing knowledge base, utilised in their concrete experience.

Methods associated with learning by doing include the use of games, simulations and role plays, visits, practical work and work experience which involves careful planning and subsequent processing.

Chapter 5 describes the organised use of work-based learning. Chapters 7, 10 and 12 describe the use of real-world tasks as the basis of group problem-solving and project work and Chapter 8 describes large-scale final year project work.

Strategy 7: Developing learning skills

Students can be passive and take a surface approach through the use of habitual study skills developed in a previous context where a surface approach was sufficient. They can also adopt a surface approach through lack of awareness of task demands. The development of study skills alone is unlikely to be effective, as most skills can be used to implement either a surface or a deep approach. However it is possible to develop learning skills in the context of developing a sense of purpose, an awareness of task demands and flexibility in adapting to different demands (Gibbs, 1981).

Skilled learners are more in control of their learning, experience greater ownership of it, and hence generate motivation. They are also more likely to process subject matter in a more active and varied way. Developing learning skills involves special 'training' type exercises (Habeshaw et al, 1989) and reflection on learning (see Strategy 4) integrated into courses and learning tasks.

Chapters 4, 5, 10, 12 and 13 all describe case studies where attention was paid to the development of the appropriate learning skills as part of efforts to improve the quality of student learning.

Strategy 8: Project work

Project work is perhaps the most common strategy used in higher education for the purpose of going beyond reproduction of information to the application of knowledge. As project work almost always involves the application of prior knowledge to problems, it emphasises the role of a sound knowledge base. Consequently project work usually takes place at the end of a course of study. Where it is used as a vehicle for learning in new areas it overlaps with problem-based learning in its methods (see Strategy 3). Where project work involves academic vehicles such as dissertations it may not involve direct experience, but it nearly always involves student activity, and students usually work more independently during project work than in other parts of their courses. Project work can be highly motivating for students, capturing a significantly greater proportion of students' time and energy than parallel taught courses of equivalent assessment value. The level of motivation seems to depend on the extent of students' responsibility for choosing and managing the project, and on the extent to which students are involved in negotiating the project's assessment. Group project work (see Strategy 5) can be particularly motivating.

Chapters 7,8,10 and 12 use projects as a major part of student learning activity. Chapter 12, for example, describes a Law course designed around six projects which students undertake, where all the teaching supports the projects and where there is no other coursework or assessment other than the projects.

Strategy 9: Fine tuning

The above eight strategies may seem to imply that radical alternatives to conventional taught courses are necessary to support a deep approach to learning. However it is possible to have a marked impact through modifications to conventional teaching methods such as lectures, seminars, student assignments, field work and laboratory work, without abandoning existing course structures. Such modifications, specifically designed to increase motivation, learner activity and interaction and to utilise a well structured knowledge base, include:

- Lectures. eg the introduction of active learning tasks and peer-group discussions into otherwise passive large lecture classes (see Chapter 6).

- Reading. eg the use of reading guides or the division of background reading between members of small student teams, followed by peer tutoring (see Chapter 12).

- Seminars. eg the use of tutor-less seminar groups in which pairs of students present seminars to groups which then peer-assess the seminar, or where students meet independently to discuss project work (see Chapter 8).

16

- Laboratory work. eg the replacement of selected tutor-designed laboratory exercises with student-designed experiments, followed by peer-review of the designs.

- Field work. eg independent student-designed fieldwork within a framework provided by a manual (see Chapter 10).

There are two questions which are central to each of these strategies:

- How are students assessed in a way which supports rather than undermines a deep approach?

- How do students get access to the subject content in a way which involves active rather than passive learning?

Assessment

Whatever strategy is used, students will be powerfully influenced by the assessment system they are working within. The design of assignments and, in particular, the criteria used in allocating marks, can have a dramatic effect on the way students approach both assessed assignments and other learning activities. Many conventional assessment methods, including essays, unseen exams and laboratory reports, allow students to take a surface approach or even implicitly encourage and reward such an approach.

Strategies for modifying the assessment assessment system which can influence students' approach include:

- involving students in the design of assessment, choice of assessment task and negotiation of criteria, for example through the use of contracts and self and peer assessment;

- integrating assessment into the learning process so that what is assessed is the total learning experience rather than a separate performance after learning has finished;

- setting assessed assignments which it is impossible to tackle on the basis of memorisation or through the repetition of algorithms or set procedures—for example tackling problems of forms not previously encountered or being asked to explain design decisions;

- setting criteria which reward understanding and penalise reproduction, and making these criteria explicit and understood;

- employing assignments which involve interaction between students, such as group project work;

- setting assessed tasks which are similar to 'real world' situations and problems;

17

- setting interdisciplinary assessed tasks and large-scale problem-solving tasks which involve the integration and application of knowledge.

The impact of assessment on students' approaches to learning is so pervasive that assessment is examined in every case study is the central issue in several.

Access to learning resources

If students are totally dependent on lecturers telling them what the content of the course is, then this will greatly limit the scope for a deep approach. All the above strategies have implications for how learning resources are selected and provided and for how students get access to these resources. If students are to learn actively then they will need material to learn from. Providing this material may involve: alternative forms of library provision, both in terms of learning material and learning spaces; the production of specially prepared printed material, audio-visual and computer packages; the development of students' information and research skills, and mechanisms for greater sharing of resources between students.

Chapters 11 and 13 describe the use of extensive packages of learning resources. Chapter 12 describes the development and use of wide-ranging research skills and Chapter 10 describes a short project to develop research skills prior to a major project which required the use of these skills. Chapters 6, 10 and 12 describe courses all of which involved extensive tutor-prepared manuals without which students could not have managed.

The use of learning packages does not automatically foster a deep approach just because students may be independent of teachers or classrooms. In the Open University, for example, a surface approach is as common as everywhere else (Gibbs et al, 1984). Furthermore there is evidence that attempts to induce a deep approach to learning packages through the use of in-text questions, and other devices which attempt to control the way students read, may have exactly the opposite effect and instead induce a surface approach (Gibbs et al 1982). While it may be necessary to provide students with alternative sources of information than lectures, and with the skills to use these sources, this alone will not guarantee improvements in the quality of learning.

With all the strategies described above it is not the method itself which fosters a deep approach but the way it is used. Group work can be used to achieve trivial and superficial learning outcomes just as individual work can. Projects can involve large quantities of 'busywork'. Study skills work can develop students' ability to memorise efficiently. What is crucial is that the strategies are implemented with the intention to foster a deep approach and with the four key features which foster a deep approach clearly in mind.

Chapter 3

The case studies

At the end of 1989 an invitation went out to Polytechnics and Colleges in the UK to propose courses to be involved in the CNAA Improving Student Learning project. A 'Briefing Paper' had been prepared outlining the theoretical framework of the project, similar to that in Chapter 1, and the intentions of the project concerning the way the case studies would be undertaken. Over 100 courses bid to be involved and over 1,000 copies of the Briefing Paper were requested. Some institutions, such as Newcastle Polytechnic, proposed a number of courses in an organised submission, but mostly individual lecturers or course teams proposed their own courses. The criteria used to select cases were:

- At what stage was the proposed innovation? If it was already well established then it would not be possible to study its introduction and it would be harder to make comparisons with what had taken place before. If the innovation was still only an outline plan or a general intention then it might prove too difficult to get under way within the time scale of the project. The project did not initiate the innovations: the motivation and the outline plans came from the innovators. The innovations selected were often about to start with plans well advanced. Some had already operated but only in a small-scale pilot, and some were in the middle of a series of progressive developments. There was not a single case study selected which started from scratch.

- Was the innovation very large scale? It was felt that very large scale innovations and very radical changes would be both difficult to implement and difficult to study within the time scale of the project. It was also felt that many innovations reported in the literature were so large and impressive that they were off-putting as they could seem quite beyond the resources and expertise of most ordinary lecturers to emulate. The cases selected should offer credible alternatives rather than unattainable perfection. Some of the courses selected involved very small scale innovations: fine tuning rather than wholesale revolution. It was felt crucial that it should seem possible to lecturers reading about the project to bring about worthwhile change through realistically modest innovations.

- Was the context of the case ideal? Accounts in the literature of successful innovations can seem unconvincing because the environment was so supportive and well resourced and because the innovations seem to require large numbers of like-minded people co-operating as a team to make it a success. Most lecturers are under resource pressures or teach more students than they would like. They work with part-time students with limited study time and with bored students with limited motivation and study skills. Their libraries are inadequate and their classrooms are less than ideal. They have limited opportunities to take time off to develop new methods. They have few allies and their colleagues are hostile to change or at best indifferent. An important criterion was that the context of the case should be realistically difficult. Several cases were selected because the environment seemed so difficult that it posed an irresistible challenge!

- What type of course and subject area was involved? The final selection of courses included a very wide range of levels: from part-time Certificates for students returning to learning to post-graduate Diplomas. Subjects included varied from engineering, business, law, geography and accounting, to oceanography, physiotherapy and graphic information design. First, second, third and fourth year courses were included. Academic and vocational courses and full-time and part-time courses were included. Courses with over 100 students and courses with small classes were deliberately selected. Both large and small institutions were included: from Newcastle Polytechnic to the Falmouth School of Art and Design. The intention was to demonstrate that the theoretical framework applied to all contexts equally well.

- What aspects of innovations were designed to foster a deep approach? Proposals were examined carefully to identify which of the four key features which foster a deep approach were involved. A grid was drawn up listing all the most promising courses on one axis and the list of strategies which embodied the key features (see Chapter 1) on the other. Most proposals were designed to embody several strategies. Cases were selected so that a full spread of strategies was involved overall. For example courses were selected to include examples of the use of learning contracts, problem-based learning, independent project work in groups and the development of students as learners. Particular attention was paid to the way assessment and access to learning resources was dealt with.

Eight courses were selected to be funded to be involved in the project. Because there were so many other potentially good cases a further 12 were invited to be involved without funding. Two of these, reported in Chapters 6 and 8, completed descriptive case studies.

Participants were invited to three residential meetings in Oxford at crucial points during the project, and they were supported by visits at other times during the case study work. While they were given guidance and support the innovators undertook their own studies. They administered the questionnaires themselves, undertook their own interviewing, and collected whatever evidence and undertook whatever analysis they thought appropriate. They did this while teaching their courses and, in many cases, developing their courses as they went along. These were not the kind of case studies where an outside researcher comes in to take a snapshot of what is going on. Instead it was 'action research'. Action research differs from undertaking case studies in several crucial respects. Table 3.1 summarises some of these differences.

The crucial point here is that research was not seen as a sterile activity undertaken by educationalists in order to make theoretical points. Research was an everyday activity undertaken by the lecturers in order to understand what was going on in their courses and to learn how to make them work better. The primary purpose of the research was to improve student learning. The kinds of activities these lecturers got up to can be undertaken by anyone wishing to engage in a more rigorous and searching process of developing their courses.

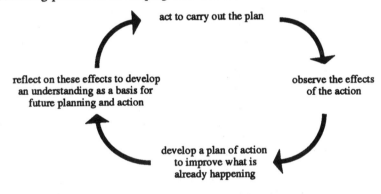

Figure 3.1: Action research cycle of activity

Action research involves a cycle of activity in four stages (Fig. 3.1). From the point of view of the Improving Student Learning project, action research had the following advantages.

- Those studying the innovations would be very close to what was happening: the project was not concerned with neutral objectivity.

- What was learnt would be able to be applied immediately, even though that would change the nature of the innovation. The project was not concerned with tightly controlled experimental comparisons of fixed alternatives.

21

Issue	Case study	Action research
When does the research take place?	After the innovation is in place, usually as a 'one shot' picture.	Throughout the process of innovation.
Who does it?	A neutral person, usually an outsider.	Those involved in the innovation.
Do the researchers implement the innovation?	No.	Yes. Those studying the innovation are those who implement it.
When does learning take place for the innovators?	Afterwards.	Throughout.
Who does the learning?	The researcher.	The innovators.
Is the innovation fixed in advance?	Yes.	No, it is modified by what is learnt through studying it, as it develops.
Whose perspective does the research take?	That of the researcher.	That of those involved.

Table 3.1: Comparison of case studies, undertaken by external researchers, and action research

- Those involved would learn and develop as teachers: the project was concerned with staff development as well as with innovation.

- Through the cyclical process of action research more progress would be made in developing teaching and assessment methods and in developing ways of monitoring the quality of student learning.

Effects of innovations on the quality of student learning were obtained in a number of ways:

- The Approaches to Studying questionnaire (see Appendix A) was used. Measures of the extent to which the students were taking a deep approach by the end of the innovation could be compared with:

- their approach at the start of the innovation or immediately before its introduction
- their approach on a parallel conventional course
- their approach on a previous conventional course
- their approach on a subsequent course, to see if the effects lasted
- the approach of other students on a parallel conventional course
- the approach of other students on the same course before it was changed.

- Students were interviewed about their approach to studying and about the features of the course which influenced their approach, especially the influence of the assessment system. Depth interviews were a vital part of the study and extracts from interviews form a major part of the case study chapters. Interviews were tape recorded or video-taped and transcripts made of what students said. Innovators were provided with sample questions to assist interviewing and help was provided in demonstrating interviewing technique and in interpreting transcripts and videos.

- Assessment results were scrutinised and the perceptions of markers and external examiners of any changes in quality were sought.

- The SOLO taxonomy was used to analyse the quality of learning outcomes.

- In several case studies students kept reflective diaries and these provided rich evidence of the quality of engagement of students with the course.

- The views of employers concerning the quality of students in the workplace was sought by several vocationally oriented courses.

- Evidence emerged from a variety of other sources, including student feedback obtained either through routine course evaluations or through specially designed evaluation studies. The innovators themselves added observations and comments.

The innovations took place between 1990 and 1991 and data was collected by the lecturers throughout this period. At a final project meeting in Oxford on September 1991 the innovators gave outline presentations in order to identify any gaps in evidence and to clarify interpretation of evidence. Collections of evidence and materials, including some fairly full reports, were handed over by December 1991. Chapters 4–13 are based on this evidence. It should be recognised that although the innovators did not write these chapters, they are based entirely on evidence provided by them, including their own interpretations and observations.

They are offered not as contributions to the research literature on student learning, but as resources for lecturers wishing to understand how to improve student learning on their courses. This is how a group of dedicated lecturers went about it, how they faced problems, succeeded and, sometimes, failed. This is the story of their endeavour. It is written to inspire and to illuminate.

Chapter 4

Supporting student learning on a part-time Business Studies course

Innovator: Julie Hartley, Birmingham Polytechnic

This case study describes mechanisms which provide students with peer support and which clarify their learning goals, implemented alongside a conventional lecture-based programme. These innovations were greatly appreciated by students but had a limited impact on their approach to studying on the course due to the nature of demands the course and its assessment still made.

Context

The innovations studied here took place in the first year of a part-time BA Business Studies course which students attend two evenings a week for three years. The course had been operating for 13 years with no significant changes in its structure, objectives or philosophy. The course had always been conventional in its delivery and most units were lecture-based and assessed by examinations. The majority of students were well-motivated adults with business experience.

Problems

The timetable was inflexible and over-full. Students attended for three hours and there was no other contact with staff and little time to attend the library. Students came in to the lectures and then went home again. Students' work and home commitments restricted their attendance and use of Polytechnic facilities. Annual monitoring of the course consistently highlighted the problems facing part-time students eg:

'Students felt neglected and commented on the lack of a clearly defined method or time for counselling or tutorial feedback.' (Annual Course Report 1985/6)

A critical review of the course in 1989 identified a number of key issues that were to influence the future design and development of the course:

- There were no mechanisms for integrating work-based learning and experience that students bring with them to the course.

- There was little interaction between students and their learning tended to be an isolated, individually focussed activity.

- Student numbers were growing rapidly and making the provision of discussion groups and adequate personal tuition even less likely.

- The course was modularised, increasing the likelihood of compartmentalised learning and an instrumental approach to collecting units rather than understanding their personal business contexts.

The following statement by a student illustrated a common attitude to study on the course:

'I have a very demanding job and I find that work often takes priority over the college. I try to keep up but very often I just read it and leave it. I haven't got the time to get to grips with the nitty gritty. My previous qualification in road transport really encouraged rote learning and I'm finding it difficult to break out of the pattern.'

This student's scores on the Approaches To Studying questionnaire at the start and end of the first year revealed a depressing deterioration in the quality of learning, with low and declining motivation, a very low and declining deep approach and a high surface approach throughout.

	Achieving	Reproducing	Meaning
Start of first year	10	21	10
End of first year	4	19	4

The course had many of the characteristics which lead to a surface approach:

- a heavy workload—students have to undertake eight units in their first year;

- high class contact hours—75 percent of time in college is spent in class, mostly in lectures.

- A lack of opportunity to pursue subjects in depth—due to the workload and work and family commitments.

- A threatening and anxiety-provoking assessment system—examinations represent 70 percent of marks and every unit contributes to the degree even in the first year.

The innovations

There were a number of innovations within units as lecturers attempted to integrate students' work experience and explore practical applications of academic concepts. However, institutional pressures for standardisation of units meant that the problem, at this stage, had to be tackled outside the existing units.

Two key innovations were introduced for the first time in the 1990/91 year: the establishment of study networks and the development of a new core unit entitled Business Workshop. It is these two innovations which are the focus of this case study. The study networks were established to encourage interaction between students and to provide peer support and motivation. The Business Workshop was designed to bring about personal development and the integration of personal business experience with academic learning though a process of reflection. It was also designed to support personal goal setting which would initiate a degree of independence within a strongly constrained course structure. Meetings with the lecturers involved were held to discuss the nature of the problems and to plan these innovations. A team of lecturers was involved as it was a large course, and a shared understanding of the problem and the methods used to tackle it was vital.

Study Networks

Study networks are a form of self-help group for students. Some students had previously informal self-help groups and this innovation formalised this arrangement for all students and provided continuing support. The aims of the study networks were:

> '... to encourage students to support each other and encourage students
> to take deep approaches to learning'.

The key feature of study networks which were intended to foster a deep approach was the provision of a positive emotional and motivational climate and the opportunity for interaction between students in independent groups.

Students were allocated to groups of six to eight on the basis of geographical location on the assumption that those living closest together would be most likely to meet outside of class. Some students subsequently changed group membership and groups were formed whose members worked for the same company or shared cultural or other values.

The formation and support of these groups involved three stages designed to encourage ownership, effective working practices and shared goals. In the first stage students were involved in team-building exercises during the induction programme.

They engaged in brainstorming to identify possible benefits of study networks and how they might exploit this potential. A typical initial network building exercise might contain the elements described in Table 4.1.

Study Network Exercise
1   An exchange of relevant information: names addresses, telephone numbers, work experience, study experience etc.
2   A discussion involving sharing of experiences and feelings about how students have managed to cope with studying in the past, survival strategies etc.
3   A simulation exercise in which students in their groups learn to share information. This exercise includes simulated 'phone calls'.
4   A brainstorm around the question: *What practical steps can we take in this study network which will help us to learn?* The outcomes of all the group brainstorms would be displayed on posters for discussion and then typed up and circulated to all the groups.
5   The creating of group action plans identifying ways in which group members are going to help each other when they are given their first assignment.

Table 4.1: A typical initial network building exercise

Stage two involved taking part in business simulation games which helped promote cohesiveness within groups. These took place during a two-day residential event which was part of the Business Workshop described below.

In stage three students focused on analysis of group processes, the understanding of group dynamics and the development of effective working practices.

Increasingly tutors on other units began exploiting the benefits of coherent groups in other aspects of the course. Study networks sometimes sat together in class or co-operated on exercises or even on assignments.

Study networks in practice

The way these study networks operated in practice is explored here by examining the results of a survey undertaken at the end of their first year of operation. Seventy percent of the first year intake responded to the questionnaire.

Ninety-two percent of students were still a member of a study network at the end of the year. Most students participated in only one study network though some (11 percent) participated in more than one. Networks varied in size, by the end of the year, from two to eight, with four and six being the most common size. No groups larger than eight survived the year that large. Three quarters of all the networks changed at least one of their members during the year.

Students contacted each other in a variety of ways and most networks used a variety of methods (see Table 4.2). Students met outside college more than within college, illustrating the difficulties they have with the tight college timetable.

		% of students
A	Phone	89
B	Personal contact outside college	79
C	Personal contact within college	64
D	Post	22
E	Other	22

Table 4.2: Question 5: How does your study network operate?

The networks were used by students for a wide range of activities (see Table 4.3).

		% of students
A	Sharing lecture notes	89
B	Distributing material provided by tutors	84
C	Sharing relevant information	77
D	Mutual support/motivation	76
E	Assignment work	69
F	Sharing administrative information	65
G	Problem solving	65
H	Discussion	53
I	Sharing books	52

Table 4.3: Question 6: What kinds of activities are evident in your study network?

Sharing information is crucial to part-time students and the study networks acted as a kind of information brokerage, supplying lecture notes, reading materials and course information.

Most networks (62 percent) met at least weekly and 95 percent of students reported finding the networks useful or very useful. Almost all students indicated that they thought the development of study networks should be encouraged on the course.

One-hour interviews were conducted with six students at their place of work to follow up their responses to the questionnaire.

The networks these students belonged to met either each week or every fortnight. The average network size was five, though attendance was variable. Networks established informal mechanisms to encourage attendance, such as planning to work on assignments or to share information regularly. Members of one network only contacted each other by phone.

Most networks became social gatherings and there was strong support for them being self-selecting as those with similar interests and values were most likely to continue successfully. Their reasons for choosing to form and continue with a network included the isolation of studying alone, overlaps of interests, race, gender or work environment, the mutual desire to help and be helped and the need for assistance with assignments.

Students saw the networks as increasing motivation and keeping each other going, and they appreciated the peer pressure against idleness. Networks were perceived as substitutes for tutors where you could get help with problems. The three stages of network formation and support described above seemed to have performed a valuable function of improving the quality and quantity of information between members early on, concerning their interests and work, and this aided group bonding. Networks were valued as an opportunity to discuss and understand, as a source of alternative perspectives which aided learning and as a creative force for the generation of ideas. They were seen to make the course more interesting.

Problems within study networks included obvious practical difficulties of meeting, especially if the members were geographically distant, difficulties of handling interpersonal problems and strong personalities, and the disruption caused if a network broke up mid-year. Not all networks had productive meetings when members had not done the agreed preparation. Building trust and commitment within networks and developing the skills to tackle difficulties seems crucial to their success.

The Business Workshop

The Business Workshop was designed to help students integrate their studies with their work experience and their personal and career goals. It was a self-development exercise which encourages students to reflect on their past experiences and use the insights gained to plan for the future. The objectives of the workshop activities were:

- To raise students' self-awareness concerning their career and life goals.

- To provide an opportunity to relate theory to business practice.

- To help individuals to identify their personal learning needs, business skills and knowledge requirements.

- To enhance the individual's life choices and potential employability during and at the end of the course.

- To provide an opportunity to consolidate individual learning.

- To help individuals develop their problem-solving and decision-making skills.

The self-development activities were split into four sections:

1. *Where are you now?* —an opportunity to audit previous experience.

2. *Where do you want to go?* —an analysis of future aspirations and objectives.

3. *How can you achieve your goals?* —the development of action plans.

4. Assessment.

Students were provided with a 40-page manual containing an outline of the workshops, instructions for 11 exercises and details of the assessment process. An extract is shown in Table 4.4.

EXERCISE NO.2
Current Skill Inventory: Strengths and Weaknesses
Skill or qualification areas can be classified under several general headings. Under each general heading below, briefly note two or three specific areas which you feel are your and two or three areas which you think are your skill areas related to your current job. Your is, of course, confidential. Don't be too modest self-critical!

	Strengths	Weaknesses
A. Professional/ Technical Skills	1. 2. 3.	1. 2. 3.
B. Social/Interpersonal Skills	1. 2. 3.	1. 2. 3.
C. Communication/ Language Skills	1. 2. 3.	1. 2. 3.
D. Administrative Skills	1. 2. 3.	1. 2. 3.
E. Personal Skills	1. 2. 3.	1. 2. 3.
Other	1. 2. 3.	1. 2. 3.

Table 4.4: An extract illustrating material to support one of the manual exercises

1. Audit of present position	1,500 word report	25 % of marks
2. The future—goals and objectives	1,500 word report	25 % of marks
3. Action planning	2,000 word report	25 % of marks
4. Presentation to peers	Presentation	25 % of marks
	Assessed by peers	

Table 4.5: Elements of the Workshop assessment

In addition to the manual, students were allocated a workshop tutor. Each tutor ran clinic-based sessions for about 30 students. Students who required a tutorial simply booked an appointment with an appropriate tutor. Students were encouraged to seek out other sources of support and guidance, for example from family, friends, work colleagues and other students.

The Business Workshop was introduced during a two day residential meeting at the start of the first term after which students were largely on their own except for the 'clinics' with tutors. The workshop was the equivalent of any other unit in assessment terms and the assessment involved four elements:

The Business Workshop in practice

Student reaction to the Business Workshop activities have been extremely positive. They found it challenging and stimulating. Many students admitted to finding it hard to reflect on what were sometimes personal and painful experiences but some who were interviewed said they considered it to be the crucial element of the course, eg:

'It gave me a vehicle to analyse myself. It made you ask "What am I? What do I want?" I began to see where I wanted to go, to explore opportunities and realised that I could change and that it was up to me to realise my own potential.'

This student showed an increase in the extent of her deep approach during the year, in marked contrast to the student described on page 25.

	Achieving	Reproducing	Meaning
Start of first year	17	20	11
End of first year	21	21	18

Material from the written reports indicated that students took the exercises and assessment very seriously and that a great deal of quality reflection took place. For example:

'By virtue of my race and class I was not totally accepted at school. This resulted in personal problems of a motivational nature. Later I was to realise that by allowing others to influence my perceptions was to deny my self belief. Having realised this I have endeavoured to dismiss the perceptions of others and to strive to accomplish all that I truly believe I can accomplish.'

This student's approaches to studying improved, from a good base. Her motivation increased, surface approach declined and deep approach increased to a very high level.

	Achieving	Reproducing	Meaning
Start of first year	17	16	19
End of first year	19	14	23

The key features of the workshops in terms of fostering a deep approach are:

- the way they help to provide a well structured knowledge base by integrating personal and academic learning;

- the extensive reflection on experience and learning;

- the interaction they engender, both with the tutors and with others, as students discuss their reflections and action plans;

- the motivation they engender as students set their own goals.

Although the other course units are fixed in content, process and timetable, students were more able to exploit the course to meet their own ends and to respond to it independently, rather than passively.

Students' approaches to learning

The effects of the two innovations on students' approaches to learning were monitored by administering the Approaches to Studying questionnaire during the induction week in October 1990 and just prior to the end of year examinations in June 1991. Sixty-four students out of 87 completed the questionnaire at the start (74 percent) and 62 out of 79 at the end (78 percent), including data for 48 students who completed the questionnaire on both occasions.

There was no change in students' motivation ('Achieving scale scores') or deep approach ('Meaning' scale scores) between the start and end of the course but their surface approach ('Reproducing' scale score) declined significantly ($t = 2.8, p < .01$).

	Achieving	Reproducing	Meaning
Start of first year	15.81	16.04	14.56
End of first year	15.25	14.60	14.69

In the past it had been assumed that the course induced a progressively more dominant surface approach and a weaker deep approach in students, as illustrated by the student on page 25. This trend appeared to have been partly reversed. In addition the second administration of the questionnaire took place just before the examinations when the Business Workshop had finished and the influence of the study networks might have been expected to have been somewhat overshadowed by the threatening demands of the conventional examinations. This may have led to students responding more to the demands, and especially the assessment demands, of their other units in the way they completed the questionnaire, which would have led to higher surface approach scores and lower deep approach scores. Certainly the evidence from the questionnaire does not correspond well with the qualitative data from interviews concerning students' learning on the Business Workshop or the way students described their learning in their study networks. This illustrates the context-dependency of the ways students approach their learning. In this course the ways students approach their other units is unlikely to be significantly effected until some of the rationale and methodology of the innovations described here imbues the rest of the course.

Approaches to Studying scores were correlated with assessment results to see which approaches were successful. None of the scores from the start of the course correlated with average marks for the whole first year, but by the end of the year there was a significant negative correlation between 'Reproducing' scale scores and marks ($r = -.29, p < .05$) and a significant positive correlation between 'Meaning' scale scores and marks ($r = +.27, p < .05$). In other words, students did better by adopting a deep approach than by adopting a surface approach.

Further developments

Students appeared to be continuing in their study networks into their second year without any support or formal arrangements. In response to evaluation data the first year students are being encouraged to choose the members for their own networks rather than being allocated to networks on the basis of geographical location. There are moves to link the individually undertaken Business Workshop to the networks so that students discuss their strengths and weaknesses and develop their action plans in their networks rather than reflecting on their own. Business Workshop tutors are being linked to networks rather than individuals and may perform more of a personal tutoring function.

The innovator, Julie Hartley, has run staff development workshops within Birmingham Polytechnic and there is now widespread interest in setting up formalised self-help networks within a wide range of part-time courses.

Key features and conclusions

In a course with significant problems of isolation and lack of discussion for part-time students the use of study networks has enabled students to interact and support each other, with negligible running costs. The introduction of the Business Workshop has introduced a major element of independent learning involving significant reflection and integration of work experience into a course where students were dependent and unreflective and where academic study linked poorly to students' prior and concurrent work-based learning. The course therefore employed three of the four key features which foster a deep approach: a motivational context, through relating to students' personal learning goals; interaction, through the study networks, and a well structured knowledge base, through the integration of students' business experience in the Business Workshops.

Despite these innovations being very positively evaluated by students, their impact on students' approaches to studying on conventional units was limited to a reduction in the extent to which they took a surface approach. Even though a deep approach led to better student performance, the conventional units still appeared not to foster a deep approach. While students' personal learning problems had been successfully addressed, the quality of their academic learning had not.

Chapter 5

Negotiated work-based learning in Hospitality Management

Innovators: Sandra Watson and Iain Marshall, Napier Polytechnic

This case study describes the way negotiated learning contracts were used to maximise learning from work placements as part of a BA Hospitality Studies with Management course. While students responded positively to the use of learning contracts and portfolios, they adopted a predominantly surface approach to their academic studies. They did not adopt a deep approach to any greater extent on return to the Polytechnic because the demands of the course were largely unchanged.

Context

The course studied here is a four-year BA Honours degree in Hospitality Studies with Management which involves a 24-week period of industrial experience in term 3 and the summer months of year 2 of the course, for 32 students. The work experience was previously arranged by the Polytechnic and the broad areas of work experience agreed by the department. Students undertook a project on one aspect of the placement which was assessed on a pass/fail basis. This work-placement was considered to be a learning opportunity which was not fully exploited. To make full use of the opportunity would take more staff time, and that would take more resources. If the placement were to have the same status as a taught component of the course then the teaching resources which a taught course would generate could be allocated to supporting the placement. The key issue here was whether the assessment of a work placement could be made sufficiently rigorous that it could justify this status.

The work placement was intended to improve the quality of student learning in the final year. The Approaches to Studying questionnaire was administered to students

35

six months before the placement to provide a baseline. Students scores, as shown below, revealed high Achieving and Reproducing scale scores. Students adopted a surface approach to a greater extent than Social Science norms would lead one to expect.

	Achieving	Reproducing	Meaning
6 months before placement n=28	14.9	15.5	14.9
Social science norms	12.7	13.6	14.2

The challenge facing the innovation was whether students could be re-oriented towards a deep approach through the revised format of industrial placement.

The innovation

The process of negotiating and assessing a work-based learning contract involved six stages:

1. Students attended workshops with staff to prepare individual learning plans.

2. Students each negotiated a learning plan with the Polytechnic assessor.

3. Students agreed their learning plan with their placement employer.

4. Students worked towards their agreed learning outcomes in their placement. Their learning contract could be reviewed and updated.

5. Students returned to the Polytechnic with evidence of the agreed learning outcomes having been achieved.

6. Evidence of achievement of these learning outcomes was presented by the student and employer for assessment.

As a prelude to Stage 1 students engaged in three one-hour group exercises in which they thought about learning from their own experience, about learning on their course, focussing on the differences between academic learning and learning from experience, and about preliminary planning for their sandwich placement. These exercises were designed to begin the cyclical process of planning, experiencing and reviewing which they would need to undertake whilst on placement. Points which consistently emerged from these workshops included the importance students placed on being actively involved in learning, the contrasting low value they placed on lectures as a way of learning, their need to see the relevance of what was being learned and their wish to have some say in what was being learned and how they might learn it. These are all features which would foster a deep approach.

The learning contract which they developed and negotiated was drawn up under five headings:

- What are you going to learn? (outcomes);

- How are you going to learn it? (resources and strategies);

- Target date for completion;

- How are you going to know that you learned it? (evidence);

- How are you going to prove that you learned it? (verification).

Students had to follow through the logic of these headings for each learning outcome they set themselves. By the time of their initial interview with their prospective employer, the students' overall objectives for learning had been developed, under three headings: course-related objectives, job-related objectives and personal objectives. To illustrate what these objectives might look like, the list below contains the kinds of learning outcomes which assessors regularly identified.

- Accomplishing the tasks involved in the placement job.

- Recognising operational problems within the work situation.

- Suggesting a strategy to overcome identified problems.

- Communicating with others as opportunities arose.

- Acknowledging the role of administration in the organisation.

- Developing skills of working with people in groups.

- Taking responsibility in a group.

- Identifying the features of a customer.

- Analysing customer needs.

- Identifying management skills from observing a role models.

- Controlling resources within an area of responsibility.

- Reacting to unpredicted situations in accordance with the policy and procedures of the organisation.

These learning outcomes statements have many similarities to the lists of management competencies developed by the National Forum for Management Education and Development (the 'Management Charter Initiative').

After their placement had been finalised students developed their personal learning plan in detail at workshop sessions in which past students, experienced in this process, and industrial placement tutors, assisted. The plan was then discussed in detail with a Polytechnic assessor, who they chose, who could negotiate changes and additions. This plan was then agreed with the employer, who tended to develop a more active role in helping students to learn, having been involved in identifying appropriate learning outcomes and in negotiating the learning agreement and the learning opportunities this involved.

Through this process of identification of learning goals it was intended that the students develop a sense of ownership and a strong commitment to achieving the goals they had set themselves.

Whilst on placement, students were required to keep a learning portfolio which included reflection on their learning experiences. They were required to collate evidence in order that they could demonstrate their learning on their return to the Polytechnic. This was a self-assessment process: students had to decide for themselves when they had learned and what would count as evidence for this learning. Their progress was monitored and supported by their placement tutor and their assessor.

On return to the Polytechnic, students were required to give a presentation to their assessor and their peers. Both their supervisor and their assessor completed an assessment sheet in relation to the initial learning plan. The headings on this sheet, reproduced in Table 5.1, demonstrate the concern for reflection and understanding in relation to each specified learning outcome, rather than for mere accumulation of industrial experience.

Assessment was based on the learning plan, the student's portfolio and the presentation.

The key features of this process which were designed to foster a deep approach in students' study within the Polytechnic are:

- the motivation which comes from students identifying their own learning goals and their own means of achieving them. There is a considerable element of independence here—more than in any other case study;

- active learning while on placement. This active learning includes not just the industrial experience but the keeping of a portfolio involving reflection on learning;

- interaction in the initial negotiation stage—with other students, supervisors, assessors and employers—with the employer and supervisor during the placement to review progress, and with the assessor afterwards in discussing learning outcomes;

- a well-structured knowledge base in that the learning plan is related to course goals as well as personal goals and job-related objectives. Work-based learning is seen as an integrated whole involving all three elements.

The study

The focus of the study was on whether the experience of negotiated learning during work placement changed the approach students took to their studies when back in the Polytechnic in their final year. Industrial placement is intended to help students

**Supervised Work-based Learning
Aid-to-Assessment Grid**

Students' Name..

Supervisor's Name..

Students' learning outcomes:

Evidence of having satisfactorily accomplished each objective:

Evidence of understanding—is the learner competent in transferring action from one situation to another?

Evidence of ability to reflect on what has happened, and add value, ie recommend an informed alternative:

Supervisor's comments:

Table 5.1: Sheet for the assessment of learning outcomes

to relate the course content to applications they have experienced, and so give the academic content more meaning. The Approaches to Studying questionnaire was administered six months before the placement, during the preparation for placement, and six weeks into the final year after students had returned from placement. A sample of students, selected to illustrate the range of approaches identified by the questionnaire, were interviewed at the time of each administration of the questionnaire, and students' portfolios were also examined to identify the nature of their reflections on learning during placement.

In students' second year, six months prior to the placements, there was evidence of a wide range of approaches. Students' Reproducing scores ranged from 9–20 and their Meaning scores from 10–20. Examples of a surface approach to at least some of students' learning were common even amongst students with high Meaning scores. For example:

> Interviewer: 'What do you generally do in a lecture?'
> Student: 'Depending on the lecture you spend time listening, sometimes you write down notes, sometimes you write up notes later... if you spend time writing notes you will not understand what is said... if you don't understand it at the beginning it's difficult to go on! And I didn't understand.
> Interviewer: 'What preparation do you do for your exams?'
> Student: 'Throughout the year not very much. I could have done more... Well I passed but I feel as though I didn't do much work... a few days before each exam I revise from the summary.'
> Interviewer: 'Do you organise your studying time.'
> Student: 'No—because if I don't feel like it it's just a waste of time, you open a book and read a bit then go on to something else—you are not taking anything in.'
> (Student's Reproducing score = 12, Meaning score = 16)

The following student defined learning in the following way:

> 'Reading something or being told something and being able to reproduce what you have learned at an appropriate time'

This is an example of a very unsophisticated understanding of what learning involves. The student showed a clear surface approach on the questionnaire also revealed a surface approach in her revision technique:

> 'Went through all my notes, made revision notes from them and then learned these off by heart. Learned all the headings off by heart.'
> (Student's Reproducing score = 19, Meaning score = 12)

The following student described a surface approach to essay preparation which involved collecting information but with little thinking:

'First thing you hit the library, look up loads of references, write them down... some are crossed off my list. I then collect all the literature in one and plough my way through it making notes of all relevant information. Then I pick out the important facts and write my essay... planning is about 10 minutes and then it's finished.'

This student was perfectly aware of different kinds of learning:

'You have got to want to go out and do it. You have got to be interested in learning... you have to be something positive to learn. It's not just taking things in.'

But she found herself studying subjects she had no interest in:

'I am doing a lot of subjects I really hate, but it's a degree that's going to get me somewhere... I am doing the degree for the results at the end, not for the interesting subjects.'

So here a surface approach was being adopted due to a lack of intrinsic motivation. The high Achieving scores of students seems to have come from a strong desire to pass rather than a strong intrinsic interest in the subject. The lack of choice and student involvement in decision-making here is an issue which the negotiated work-based learning contracts was designed to address.

One student described some lecturers treating students as though they were in a production line, suggesting that there was generally little encouragement for developing their own interests. Some aspects of the course, for example the tutorials and laboratory work, did seem to encourage a deep approach and an opportunity to explore ideas. The interviews revealed students taking a surface approach to some parts and a deep approach to others, for example:

'Lab work and tutorials give me a deeper understanding.'

However the method of assessment allowed students to succeed by regurgitating lecture notes. Students, as in the example above, described exam preparation as involving little more than condensing lecture notes. As so often the assessment demands seemed to over-ride the possible positive impact some of the teaching methods might have had.

Overall the course was not succeeding in fostering a widespread and consistent deep approach.

Students were interviewed during the period in which they were preparing for their placement. This was the first occasion in which students used words like 'think' in relation to their studies or described their own interests as opposed to describing how they were responding to the demands of the course:

'Got you thinking about what you wanted to get out of the work placement by discussing in groups, especially for course-related and personal related (objectives).'

Some students identified a quite different approach to learning than elsewhere in their course. For example the following student showed a low and declining deep approach on the questionnaire which was not at all evident in relation to preparation for the placement.

'... that (the learning plan) has been very helpful—filling in the sheets made me think. The idea is a good one, to get your ideas straight before approaching employers. When I produced my learning plan I impressed myself with what I wanted to learn!'

However students who had been taking a surface approach even went about the development of a personal learning plan in a superficial way:

'It's a good thing you get marks for it or otherwise you would say "what's the point?" '.
(Student's Reproducing score = 21)

Students generally commented favourably on their learning whilst on placement:

Interviewer: 'Has the development of your own learning plan been helpful?'
Student: 'Yes. It would have been easy for me not to do very much for college work as I was working long hours. But once I started my learning portfolio I found it helped... by having to analyse problems and situations. I found I really enjoyed writing it.'
Interviewer: 'How did your learning portfolio assist your learning?'
Student: 'It helped me focus my learning, for example, by having to write about the history of the hotel, the changes in the hotel and how the summer business was mainly made up of tours. Without it I wouldn't have learnt the things I did in detail.'

When students came back from placement this learning continued:

'I really enjoyed the oral presentation. It gave me the opportunity to share my experience with other people, which was beneficial to me as well.'

Students also commented that they expected their portfolio to help them in their final year studies:

'It has taught me to focus on the important and positive parts of the course and in the future to organise myself and my course work.'

'It will enable me to stand back and assess what my aims are objectively. It will also mean that I will be able to focus on a particular subject and organise myself for course work and exams.'

Students' approach to their learning, as measured by the Approaches to Studying questionnaire, was no different in the period during preparation immediately before the placement than six months before. After students returned from placement, six weeks into their final year, their Reproducing score had dropped significantly ($p <$ .05) but their Meaning score was unchanged.

	Achieving	Reproducing	Meaning
Before placement (n = 28)	15.1	16.7	14.4
After placement (n = 26)	14.7	14.8	13.7

Table 5.2: Mean scores for students on the Approaches to Studying questionnaire before and after industrial placement

Given the radically different nature of demands on students which the work placement made, this apparent lack of improvement in students' deep approach requires some explanation. One possibility is that the Approaches to Studying questionnaire is inappropriate for identifying students' use of work experience in making sense of course material. It certainly contains items which assume a relatively conventional pattern of teaching and learning, including lectures and teacher-set tasks, and focuses attention on academic content. However, this was exactly the context students were studying in at the times they were surveyed. The questionnaire may have given a perfectly accurate indication of the way they were studying while at the Polytechnic. Students' academic courses were relatively unchanged and their approach to studying them was also relatively unchanged. The innovators commented:

'... when they returned (from placement) they slipped back into the Polytechnic-based roles which are often rather passive.'

While students said they had gained confidence in their own abilities while on placement they felt they could not use this new confidence when back in college:

'... it's completely different here because I have no responsibilities. There is no need to take decisions here so I can regress. I would like to have more responsibility, but how?'

The interviews in the final year revealed a similar range of pressures inducing a surface approach as in the second year. As before, students were able to distinguish between different types of learning but still described themselves as adopting a surface approach. For example this student defined what learning meant to him:

'Something coming from my own experience. Not just listening to lectures or reading books—that doesn't stick.'

And yet he also described his experience of the final year in the following way:

Interviewer: 'How do you prepare for exams?'
Student: ' ... cramming at the end.'
Interviewer: 'What helps you learn?'
Student: 'Revision lectures—a copy of the exam paper! ... we get too
much coursework to allow us to learn—it gets forgotten very quickly.'

The above student's Meaning score declined from 14 in the year 2 to 11 in the year three. The exams dominated many students' thinking and studying. The following student's Meaning score declined from 17 in year two to 3 in year three, but her high Achieving score (17) is reflected in her highly organised and diligent surface approach.

'I go through all my lecture notes and cut them down into short note
form. I take notes from books and break these down so that I can learn
headings. I look at past exam papers and work through examples. I think
I can identify a format which is the same in all exams.'

The following student, who did not take a surface approach (Reproducing score = 12) talked about how he had enjoyed the placement and the freedom in learning it had given him. He described a changed conception of learning since his placement, which had made him see the importance of experience. He found the final year didn't take this experience sufficiently into account:

'I want the course to take real live problems from the industry and help
us to learn from dealing with them. I want to have more of a choice in
selecting what I study on the course.'

Despite this attitude he did not take a deep approach (Meaning score = 12). The demands of the course seem to have overridden his intentions.

The following student had described gaining a great deal from her learning plan and her portfolio during her placement and having enjoyed both writing the portfolio and giving her presentation on her return, but when she was asked how the portfolio would benefit her approach to the rest of the course it was a different picture:

'Oh, I do not know. I suppose that it should but I feel so demotivated.
Nearly all our lecturers appear unenthusiastic this year. Nobody seems
to enjoy lecturing.'

Her intrinsic motivation whilst on placement was replaced by a passive reliance on motivation by others on the course.

Tutors started recognising this problem. One tutor reported recognising that placements were more important than he had thought and started attempting to involve students more in their learning while in the Polytechnic and drawing on their experiences during class work.

Conclusions

The innovation involved a considerable degree of student independence within a well worked out framework and appears to have succeeded in generating more purposeful and effective learning from the work placement. By setting their own learning goals students were more motivated to achieve them. Students seem to have reflected on their learning to a greater extent, through the use of their portfolios. The assessment process involved them actively in judging the nature and extent of their learning. Students reported gaining in confidence and maturity through this process. There was no comparable data from a work placement scheme which did not use learning contracts, but the description given by students was nevertheless very largely positive.

The impact on students' learning on the rest of their studies in college was another matter. Students started with high Reproducing scores. While students varied considerably in their approach, and appeared to approach different aspects of the course in different ways, the overall impact of the course seemed to be to induce extrinsic motivation—a desire to pass and gain a qualification—rather than any intrinsic interest in the subject matter. While on average students took a surface approach to a lesser extent in their final year than in their second year (though still higher than national norms) they did not adopt a deep approach to any greater extent. Some final year students revealed a decline in the quality of their learning and a dramatic change for the worse in their approach compared with their learning associated with the work placement. The volume of coursework, uninspiring lectures, lack of choice concerning what was learned and the demands of the exams were the most commonly implicated factors.

This is an example of a locally successful innovation having only a limited general impact because the remainder of the course was unchanged and made quite different demands on the students. This is a pattern repeated in several of the other case studies. There were signs that some lecturers were realising that students' work experience could be brought into the final year teaching to a greater extent. However, there was little sign of appropriate changes in the teaching methods, increases in the extent of student choice, independence or active involvement, or re-thinking of the nature and demands of the assessment system. Without these changes there seems little likelihood that the positive impact of the negotiated work-based learning would carry over into improving the quality of student learning in the rest of the course.

Chapter 6

Encouraging active learning In structured lectures

Innovator: Alan Jenkins, Oxford Polytechnic

This case study illustrates fine tuning of teaching methods to improve the quality of student learning. It describes the way in which three-hour lecture sessions were used to involve students in a variety of learning activities and the impact this had on students' learning outside class.

Context

The course studied here is an introductory one-term module in human geography which is part of a joint honours degree. For the great majority of students this is their first term in higher education. Over the past 15 years the course has been gradually but substantially changed. The course used to be taught mainly by conventional lectures in which the teacher spoke without interruption. The lectures were changed to what are here called structured lectures. The lecture time is broken up into short segments in some of which the teacher talks. But for much of the session students, in groups of two to three, work on tasks defined by the lecturer. Originally developed for classes lasting the conventional 60 minutes, this method has been adapted to three hour sessions for very large classes. A number of parallel innovations supported the impact of these sessions.

Previous methods, and problems

An undergraduate geography course used to employ conventional lectures to deliver course material. There were 50-60 students in the class, which took place in a banked lecture theatre with fixed rows of benches and poor acoustics. Students experienced difficulty in attending for a full 55 minutes. It was difficult for them to ask questions and difficult for the lecturer to answer questions, in such a large class. As a result students were largely passive, and used the lecture as a means of recording the lecture content. Many of the students came straight from other classes. They also went from the lecture straight into other classes and seemed not to use or think about their notes afterwards. A seminar in which the lecture was discussed took place some days later and it was clear that students had not thought about the lecture content to any great extent.

The course material covered a wide diversity of material. There was a list of suggested reading, which clearly few students read, but no set text was used as none could be found that matched the diverse approaches introduced in the course.

Most if not all students passed the course, but exam answers indicated that many students had learnt a limited amount of factual material but had great difficulty in grasping the more theoretical issues. These were precisely the areas the staff thought most important to the students' intellectual development and to their future studies in the geography department.

Over the years student numbers increased from 50–60 students to 100–120 and the amount of staff time that could be devoted to the course, particularly in informal discussions and tutorials, had to be cut.

The innovation

Students had been too busy recording information to have time to think about the content of the lecture. Consequently, key information is now provided in a course guide, which also gives students more detailed guidance on reading sources, and also in handouts provided at the start of the lecture. Students are now expected to obtain much of the course content outside of the lecture from a compulsory textbook. In addition the amount of factual material the course attempts to cover has been cut. Rather, emphasis is placed on approaching and understanding the same material from a variety of methodological positions.

Students had been largely passive in the previous conventional lectures and so problems, questions and discussion tasks are introduced into the lectures in a way which requires them to actively process the ideas presented. For each session there is a six–ten page handout which provides:

- a framework for students to add brief notes;

- extracts from books and newspapers;

- instructions for the more complicated tasks.

Tasks requiring limited instruction are explained by the lecturer and displayed on an overhead projector transparency. An example of one such structured lecture is shown in Table 6.1. To tackle the problem of rapidly declining student attention, periods of presentation are limited to a maximum of 15 minutes. Too much emphasis had been placed by students on taking notes simply to record information. Some of the tasks set in the lecture therefore use the notes the students take, or require them to write notes in response to questions. Some of the tasks students are set require them to apply ideas to new situations and to discuss ideas, so preparing them better for seminars. Students are required to bring the textbook to class and tasks are set that require them to analyse the text and guide their reading the text outside the classroom. In general students are set tasks which model the ways they should be learning independently outside class.

As students come direct from other classes it is important to spend time at the beginning of sessions recalling and processing what had been dealt with in the last lecture or seminar or in reading since the last lecture. As students could not be guaranteed to actively rehearse or use the ideas from the lecture immediately afterwards, such learning activity is now built into the lecture time.

Introducing the method

The methods described above were introduced gradually over a period of several years. Initially short breaks and quick tasks were introduced, then discussion tasks, and finally a range of larger problems. Printed support material also developed over time from occasional handouts to a substantial course guide and a substantial handout for each class session.

The main problems for the lecturer were those of fear of loss of control, especially when the noise level soars as sixty pairs of students discuss an interesting question. This fear dies away with the repeated experience of regaining control and from seeing that when the tasks are well-designed students will work purposefully. A second problem is that concerned with the necessity to 'cover the syllabus'. It is not possible to present as much in structured lectures as in conventional lectures. However, the lecturer's previous subjective experience of 'covering' the material in lectures was clearly not mirrored by students' experience of 'covering' the material! Encouraging active learning in lectures also involves thinking about students' active learning outside of lectures and cutting down the content of the course to that which can realistically be dealt with in depth. Content also needs to be seen as including intellectual skills such as problem-solving, which are developed through class activities. In time it becomes apparent that students picked up the breadth of coverage outside class, mainly through increased reading, and that the quality of understanding was greatly improved.

In the first lecture of this kind which the students experience, students are shown a graph representing the plunging attention and performance of students over an hour-long lecture, and asked to discuss, in groups of two-three what they think this graph represents. The reason for breaking up lectures and introducing activities is then explained. Each time a task is introduced, the purpose of the task is outlined. Students quickly get used to working in this way. Videos of the students during their first experience of this kind were recorded in order to examine their reactions and behaviour. They showed that even those who seemed bemused and not at all engaged at the start were working effectively by the end of their first structured lecture. Students quickly learned to sit together in twos and threes so that they could get down to the discussion tasks quickly. Not all students joined in enthusiastically. There were always some who worked in a desultory fashion at the tasks and discussed irrelevant issues.

It can be difficult to pitch the questions and tasks at the right level. If tasks are easy or have correct answers then they tend to be answered very quickly with little thought or discussion. If they are too open-ended or difficult then they may be hard for students to get going on or to finish in the time available. Also, if students think that the lecturer will answer the question anyway, they may wonder what is the point of working hard on it. Devising engaging tasks and questions and presenting them as worth the effort of tackling, is a subtle and skillful business. Walking around the classroom and discussing points with students encourages their engagement with the tasks. This is easier in a flat-floored room with gangways between seating, but is still possible in tiered lecture theatres.

The method was originally introduced in the conventional one hour timetable slot. The lecturer's subjective judgment was that time period enabled him to develop students' understanding of a central theme and for students to be actively involved throughout the session. Later the modular course of which this module was a part moved to a timetable involving three-hour slots. This would have made conventional lectures even less effective and so structured lecture format was adapted to these longer slots. As students got used to the method the lecturer found he could introduce longer and more complicated tasks requiring student groups to work largely independent of him. However, student evaluations reinforced his judgment that students found it was difficult to concentrate for this period in a structured lecture. The method seemed to work better in the conventional one hour slot.

Structured lectures in practice

Table 6.1 shows an analysis of the method in a three hour session. This is the first class session in an introductory year one course on Britain's changing geography. The role of the session was to introduce students to the course themes and to the way they are expected to learn in the structured lectures. As is shown, the session had 16 key sections. Ten of these were tasks totalling 95 minutes. There were six periods of lecturing totalling 65 minutes. No period of lecturer talk lasted more than 15 minutes and most lasted no more than 10 minutes. There was also a 20 minute break.

This session was videotaped and was used to prompt students who were interviewed on their reactions to the method, as described in Table 6.1.

It is important to emphasise that the final session of lecturer talk introduced a task students were to do outside class. The lecture handout gave precise instructions as to what students should do. The lecturer emphasised that next week's session would require them to use what they had learned from that task and that further group work would be based on it. He explained that the follow-up group task would be incomprehensible to those who had not done the work.

The lecturer knew these students would initially be confused and even angry in the

Minutes	*Lecturer or student activity*
0–10	**Task** on OHP directs students as they enter to pick up course guide, a 9-page lecture handout and to re-arrange the seating so they can sit in groups of 2–3 and get to know each other.
10-15	**Task** requires student groups to decipher graphs showing decline of student attention in a conventional lecture and the impact on student attention of the structured lecture used in the course.
15–25	**Lecturer** gives his interpretation of the graph and uses it to explain how the course will be taught and what he expects them to do in class sessions.
25–35	**Task** requires groups to interpret a quote from Wittgenstein and explain its relevance to geography.
35–45	**Lecturer** analyses the quote and shows its relevance to the course themes which are set out in the course guide.
45–55	**Task** requires individuals to write answers to questions on the lecture handout. The questions require them to draw on their commonsense knowledge of Britain's changing geography.
55–65	**Task** requires individuals to compare answers.
65–80	**Lecturer** draws on what he has overheard but his analysis takes it beyond commonsense knowledge. Using student statements he shows that it is possible to give very different interpretations of Britain's geography.
80–90	**Task** to write the quote from Wittgenstein in student's own language and explain its relevance to the course. They are warned the lecturer will not go over this task and the course guide shows them that it was on last year's exam.
90–110	**Students and lecturer take a break.**
110–120	**Task** requires students to analyse a set of quotes that give contrasting definitions of geography as a discipline and emphasise very different processes as explaining geographic patterns.
120–130	**Lecturer** interprets these quotes and links back to the quote from Wittgenstein.
130–140	**Task.** Lecture handout includes part of the introduction to the course text book. Task requires students to analyse the authors' view of geography, which processes the authors will emphasise and which they will neglect.
140–150	**Lecturer** reiterates the text's central viewpoint and introduces alternative perspectives.
150–160	**Task** to analyse a brief extract from a book with a contrasting interpretation.
160–170	**Task** which requires students to write a summary of the whole session.
170–180	**Lecturer** emphasises the role of the textbook in the course and introduces a Task which requires them to work outside class to answer questions relating to the first chapter. They are told next week's session will be based on these answers.

Table 6.1: Analysis of a 3–hour structured lecture

session. However he believed this was a stage they had to go through to appreciate what was required of them in and outside class. From experience he knew that most of them would soon understand and appreciate what was required of them.

During the second structured lecture he drew further attention to one of the messages in the course guide:

> 'You will not get many detailed notes or much factual material from these sessions. Such information is very important but I think you can learn that better by reading. In particular you are required and assumed to be getting that information from the text book.'

Deep and surface approaches in geography

Contemporary human geography is concerned with describing and analysing the pattern of activities on the earth's surface—and with explaining those patterns emphasising the role of social, economic and political processes. Since the 1970's a variety of methodologies have been championed as prime explanatory factors. Spatial analysis with its emphasis on the role of positive economics, Marxist and neo-marxist approaches and structuralist methodologies have profoundly effected research and course content.

This course seeks to introduce students to some of these approaches. It takes as its central idea a quote from Wittgenstein:

> 'Whatever we see could be other than it is.
> There is no a priori order of things.'

These ideas are presented and analysed in the context of changes to the human geography of Britain since 1970—a period of significant geographic change which has spawned considerable academic controversy. Even though most of the students have studied geography at 'A' level these ideas are generally new and often troubling for them. They tend to view knowledge as relatively fixed and expect geography to be a relatively factual subject largely concerned with descriptive knowledge about regions.Their explanations for the location of phenomena tend to emphasise vaguely-understood physical and economic factors.

Students' comments on course evaluations emphasised that at school they were used to the teacher and the textbook as being the source of authoritative statements and used to teaching methods which involved the teacher telling them things. Many commented that they were used to dictated notes and assessment methods emphasising descriptive factual knowledge. What the course sought to do was to move away from surface approaches to deep approaches to the course content and to knowledge.

Students who took a surface approach would look for and describe a geography of Britain that was unproblematic and which essentially required them to learn a set of descriptive factual statements about the location of iron and steel plants, the new service industries and so on. They not only would have little understanding of the processes explaining these patterns but would expect these explanations to be authoritative facts. Students who took a deep approach would expect to find alternative explanations of these patterns, would analyse authors and the teacher for their particular interpretations and seek to build their own understanding of the methodological approaches and of Britain's changing geography. Furthermore students who had fully taken a deep approach would be able to take these ideas of alternative and competing methodologies and apply them to other disciplines and to their understanding of their everyday world.

The impact of structured lectures

No before and after study was conducted because the changes were introduced gradually over a period of some years. It was also not easy to compare the module with parallel modules because a range of innovations were also being used in other geography modules. The evidence from regular annual evaluation studies and from interviews with students is that more of them take a deep approach to the course material. This is despite a doubling of the number of students than when the course started. What is remarkable is that eighteen months after the course ended students vividly recalled the impact of structured lectures on their approach to the class sessions and to the course.

Fifteen years of regular course evaluation feedback has revealed a consistent pattern of student response. Initially students find the method confusing. They look for hard facts and for the lecturer's interpretation and they don't get them. They do get a few facts, and they sometimes get the lecturer's interpretations of facts, but not until after they have made their own interpretations. They start to realise that they can't sit back and expect the lecturer to sort everything out for them. A student said:

> 'This is different, it's demanding ... you have to work on it ... a lot is expected of you but you soon get the hang of it'.

Early assignments show a continued tendency to focus on detail and repetition. Later on they realise that they have to find factual information outside class and use this to support ideas which have been developed in the lectures. They report that lectures make them think as if they were in a small group and contrast this with how they operate in conventional lectures on other courses they take, where they are concentrating on note-taking and sometimes on dictation.

A later assignment requires them to take a very densely written textbook and to use the evidence in it to write an article for a sixth form geography journal on the changing geography of Britain. By requiring them to write it for school level students this encourages them to write in language and using ideas they understand. In the past, written work had shown that students were quite adept at reproducing, with minor changes in wording, what they had read. However, the lecturer doubted they understood much, and examination answers and seminar discussions generally confirmed this fear. In contrast their articles for this later assignment showed a clear emphasis on possible explanations of change, gained from the lectures and backed up by evidence from the textbook, rather than on unprocessed factual evidence used to describe change.

No systematic study has been made of the impact of the method on the work students produce or the quality of students' examination answers. The lecturer's subjective impression is that the changes introduced, and in particular the structured lectures, have significantly improved the quality of students' assignments and the quality of examination answers. The exam focuses on a limited area of content. In the lecturer's judgment, he can now ask quite complex questions in the exam which, to be answered well, require a sophisticated understanding of the course themes. Overall he judges more students show they have taken a deep approach to the course themes.

Annual evaluations confirm to the lecturer his impression that, for the majority of students, these changes push them to take a deeper approach. Particularly interesting are these comments in response to the question:

'What advice would you give someone who is just about to start the course next year?'

'Don't be shocked by the tremendous difference in lecture technique. By the end, no matter how confused you were at first, you do seem to understand the information.'

'A relatively small subject has been gone into detail and seen from a variety of perspectives with the central issues repeated, so as to emphasise them. The subject is also very open to argument and you are left to argue your own views, instead of just learning a load of facts like at 'O' and 'A' level.'

'Take part in the lectures as much as possible. Read around the subject. Don't take this course if you just want to sit there and be given notes.'

To complement these annual evaluations five students were interviewed 18 months after they had taken the module. All the students had passed the module and had continued to study geography. Their grades in the course ranged from a C to an A. They were asked a about a variety of issues centering on how the course was taught and in particular on whether the method of lecturing affected how they had tried to learn the course material. During the interview they were shown sections of a video that had been made of the first lecture in the module; the session described above. The interviews confirmed that the method of lecturing pushed students to take a deep approach to their studies. In particular, students contrasted how the approach changed their behaviour and intentions in comparison to the traditional lecture. They could identify clearly what learning meant in this course. It was clear that without any prompting from the video the students could vividly remember the overall impact of the class sessions and even describe details of particular sessions.

All of the students were used to conventional lectures. Most had been accustomed to them at school. All were receiving traditional lectures in some of their other courses. Though they appreciated that they got more facts from the conventional lecture they were all critical how it affected their approach to studying:

'It was always the teacher talking at us and us just sitting there and taking notes. (Our role) was just to sit there and listen. Many times we just sat there doodling in our books. You were just learning textbook theories and what the teacher told you.'
(A student describing a class of seven)

One student's experience at school was essentially similar. When asked what 'learning' meant in that context she commented:

'Sort of parrot-fashion revising or remembering what the notes were. When you had to go and write an essay, then you would get a number of textbooks and sort of draw them together, but most of all it was what the teacher gave you. That was the correct answer and you just kind of regurgitated it all out.'

Commenting on other lectures at the Polytechnic a somewhat similar pattern emerged. A student reported that:

'The lecturer was just passing on information. You were expected to digest that information, write it down so you'd got some kind of notes. (Learning there) was taking in the information. I suppose you accept it. That's what you are supposed to be learning. I don't think you really question too much what is being said to you.'

Another student looked back to the history course at a university he had started some ten years ago. There the lectures were:

'... very traditional. It was assumed you had a sort of empirical background knowledge of what the lecturer was going to talk about, which certainly wasn't really the case. It was assumed that you'd done masses of reading, which of course you never do, as you don't have the time let alone the inclination... I suppose effectively I was trying to take as many notes as possible.'

All the students saw the structured lectures as significantly affecting the way they approached the lecture sessions and the course as a whole, even though most were initially bewildered as to what was expected of them:

'I used to find it a bit, maybe not exhausting, but you were always kept on your toes. We're going to have to listen to this, 'cos we're going to have to talk about this, and then maybe explain it to him when he comes around again. We had actually got to think for ourselves. You've got to draw your own conclusions which may or not be wrong, but then you might be told the right answer if there is one. You're also learning how to think as well. You are exercising the brain as you go along rather than taking in the facts, maybe thinking about the facts... also processing them. You're actually forced to!'

Students appreciated having a lecture handout setting out the structure of the session, with both detailed information and space to add their own notes. A student observed:

'All the key ideas were there and you could listen more and form your own ideas as time went along. You actually had a chance to understand what was going on and not just think,"Oh God! Ive got to get this down really quickly otherwise I might miss it".'

Looking back at the notes he had taken in the course a student said:

'They were about issues ... reminders to myself about maybe angles I had not thought about, or maybe specific points I hadn't thought of. You ended up with an understanding, not necessarily just a written record, but an understanding of some of the issues involved.'

Assessment and student learning

The assessment system was seen as supporting the approach of the structured lectures and the overall course objectives. Students' first assignment required them to take a long complicated theoretical article and present it's central arguments as a two page popular newspaper article. One student looked back at how she had approached that assignment:

'Then to me it was just getting in as much information is as possible. I was getting every figure I could find. Other people were putting it into their own words. They'd leave out a lot of the stuff but they would get the idea in and that was what was wanted. Looking at it now, it is really strange how I did it.'

Her comments on how she revised for the exam are also revealing. She expected, correctly, that as with the previous year's paper there would be a question that required them to use the quote from Wittgenstein. The question required them to take the quote and 'explain to someone who has not taken this course how it exemplifies certain of the course's central themes'. Considering how she had gone about preparing for the exam she mused:

'It's really strange... I remember you going over that in lectures so for the exam I was looking through my notes and what people had said and considering what I thought and what you had said, trying to get an idea of exactly what it meant, and I think I did, just about.'

Another student saw the exam as:

'Requiring you to show that you had an understanding of the issues involved, based to some extent on hard facts, but not on the hard facts alone. You have got to be able to demonstrate that you are able to argue a case or to show that you understand the arguments for a case. The idea that there was more than one opinion about something, more than one approach, that definitely had to come across in the exam. No particular party line on anything. I wouldn't necessarily toe them anyway. But I would be aware that if I wasn't going to toe them, I was going to have to give specific reasons why I wasn't. Certainly the exam was closely related to the course.'

From these interviews the lecturer felt confident that structured lecturing encouraged students to take a deep approach to their studies and that the methods of assessment supported that goal.

Structured lecturing in large classes

Evaluation of the use of the method by the same lecturer in an introductory class of about 500 students in a North American University revealed students to be evenly split between those who loved it, those who were neutral and those who hated it. It proved difficult for a single lecturer to manage alone and teaching assistants found it difficult to help. One factor that may have been significant in this rather different response is that in Britain many of the students attended an intensive residential weekend designed to make relationships between students, and between lecturers and students, more open. In contrast in America there was a lack of such a trusting relationship and the students were taught by others when in smaller groups. Given the difficulty of setting appropriate questions and tasks, this lack of rapport may have been crucial. In such a large group it is also difficult to get in amongst students to stimulate discussion and to listen. It is too easy for students to hide and not be active. Interaction between students is crucial to active learning in such settings.

However, perhaps the key reason the method was not so successful is that, as a visiting lecturer, the lecturer had no control over the method of assessment. This was entirely by multiple choice objective questions which largely emphasised factual recall of information and which were written by another member of staff. The lecturer suspected this fitted into students' expectations of what learning was required of them and most could therefore see little point to the tasks that he set. This experience strongly reinforced his view that it is essential to ensure that the assessment system is congruent with the teaching methods and encourages the higher level learning goals that structured lectures can develop. This point is vital to understanding some of the difficulties experienced in other case studies where the assessment was unchanged or out of the control of the innovator. In particular the innovation described in Chapter 9 suffered from an incompatible assessment system.

Guidelines for structured lectures

The purpose of the method is to make learning active both in lectures and outside class during independent study. Class time is used to model how students should approach material.

- Lecturing should be limited to short bursts.

- After or before each short burst of lecturing, brief learning tasks should be introduced, involving the application of principles and discussion between students in twos and threes.

- The learning tasks work best if they are varied in format and process, engaging, open-ended, but possible to tackle and discuss in a few minutes.

- As students (and the lecturer) become used to the method it is possible to introduce much longer and more open-ended tasks.

- It is necessary to provide handouts, course guides or guides to reading, so that course material is accessible to students outside the lecture.

- Activities should be related to, and introduce students to, the major learning activities which they will undertake outside class.

- It is important to explain the rationale of the method to students, and to explain the purpose of tasks carefully.

- It is essential that the assessment system reinforces students orientation to a deep approach that the structured lectures encourage.

- Good social relationships between students, and between students and the lecturer, certainly help. If students work in small groups in seminars or project groups outside the lecture then it helps if they sit in the same groupings in the lecture. Without such existing social patterns, and in otherwise impersonal courses, the method can help to establish good relationships.

- The method works well with large groups (over 100) but it can be difficult to make it work well with very large groups (over 400).

- It is sensible to introduce the method gradually as the teacher gains confidence, builds up support material for the class sessions and learns when to insert tasks, and what kinds of tasks are effective.

- In the early development of using the method the class session is essentially a lecture with a few breaks for small activities. As one gains confidence and belief in the approach the class takes on the form of a workshop with little or no resemblance to the conventional lecture.

Key features and conclusions

This case study has described extensive fine-tuning of a conventional method—the lecture—within a relatively unchanged course structure. The key features are those of learner activity and interaction in what would otherwise have been a passive situation involving no interaction. Other congruent fine-tuning changes in the course, especially in the assessment system, supported the impact of this fine-tuning. In other case studies, such as that in Chapter 9, fine-tuning was much less successful because their were no such congruent changes in the course context. On its own fine-tuning, particularly in classroom practice, may have a limited impact without parallel changes in other features of the course, and in particular the assessment demands.

Further reading

Bligh, D. (1981) *What's the use of Lectures?* Harmondsworth, Penguin.

Gibbs, G. and Jenkins, A. (1984) *Break up your lectures, or Christaller sliced up.* Journal of Geography in Higher Education. Vol.8. No.1. pp 27-39.

Gibbs,G., Habeshaw,S. and Habeshaw,T. (1989) *53 Interesting things to do in your lectures.* Bristol: TES.

Jenkins, A. (1992) *Active learning in structured lectures.* In A.Jenkins and G.Gibbs (Eds.) *Teaching Large Classes*, London: Kogan Page.

Chapter 7

Problem-based learning in Automotive Engineering Design

Innovator: Peter Griffiths, Coventry Polytechnic

This case study describes a comprehensive problem-based learning approach to the second year of a BEng course. It was possible to compare the course with the first year and the second year of a conventional parallel course and to monitor the longer-term effects on students' approaches to studying. As well as demonstrating dramatic changes in the quality of students' learning the case study illustrates the value of staff development in supporting significant change.

Context

The BEng Automotive Engineering Design is a four year sandwich course with the first year common with a conventional BEng Mechanical Engineering degree. The approach in years two and four is completely new and intended to develop engineering design skills. The focus of this case study has been on year two, in which students first encounter a problem-based approach. In the first year the course is a relatively conventional pattern of lectures and practicals assessed by individually undertaken coursework and unseen exams. Students enrol having selected whether to take the conventional course or to take the Automotive Engineering Design route. In the year the case study was undertaken about 50 students took the Mechanical course and 30 took the Automotive course. The following year about 60 took each route.

Students' learning on the conventional BEng

Students completed the Approaches to Studying questionnaire in May 1990 at the end of their first year. Table 7.1 compares those students who had chosen to go on to study Mechanical Engineering in the second year with those who had chosen to study the problem-based Automotive Design Engineering course, and also includes the national norms for science students.

	Achieving	Reproducing	Meaning	Exam
Students choosing Mechanical Engineering	16.00	16.68	14.34	61.4%
Students choosing Automotive Engineering	14.50	16.25	15.66	56.7%
Science student norms	13.08	14.26	13.93	

Table 7.1: Mean scores on the Approaches to Studying questionnaire and exam marks in the first year

There were no significant differences between the two groups of students. Whatever differences subsequently emerged in the second year could not be attributed to the students having a different approach to learning to start off with. The assessment results were also examined to see if those students choosing the problem-based Automotive Engineering Design course scored any better. In fact the students going on to the Mechanical Engineering second year gained, on average, marks nearly five percent better, though this difference was not significant due to the wide range of marks in both groups.

Both groups scored significantly higher on the 'Reproducing' scale than the norms for science students ($p < .01$). In other words students took a surface approach to the first year to a greater extent than one might have expected.

Students were also interviewed before they started the second year about the way the had studied in the first year. While there were examples of students taking a deep approach the following extracts from the interviews illustrates what the data from the questionnaire shows: a surface approach was widespread.

> 'The phase test was coming up and nobody understood it ... we were all doing the same old trick of learning it parrot-fashion just to get through the test which was coming up... the lecturer understood it but nobody in the class did.'

> 'I felt the learning took place afterwards when you went to use it—you sit in class and laboriously learn about this, this and this—but really learn about it out at work.'

> 'I liked Materials—it's easy—just information.'

> 'The whole process is concentrating on gathering a great jumble of information ... I gathered 20 pages of notes taken straight from books, most of it waffle ... just gathering information.'

'If I'm not interested I do the minimum to scrape through—leave things to last minute panic revision for the exam'

It wasn't simply the information which students approached learning in this way. The way they went about tackling problems also illustrated a surface approach which involved a thoughtless following of fragments of algorithms rather than any strategy based on understanding:

' ...read the question—get an answer—get it right—start another—get it wrong, check units etc.—if I still can't do it, leave it, come back later—usually can't see the wood for the trees'

' ...got the notes out and tried to plough through it...I just copied down not understanding it...working backwards to see where the numbers come from...going through worked examples trying that again ...'

'I tried to suss out an easy way to do it—asked for help—was told how and followed instructions.'

Even if students did reasonably well they were sometimes aware that their learning had not been effective:

'(My) pattern of study has not developed. I didn't seem to remember anything. I'd come second in the exam but I still wasn't overly sure of the whole subject. I knew what we had to understand but I didn't understand how—my background knowledge wasn't adequate.'

This student adopted a surface approach to a considerable extent, as confirmed in the pattern of scores on the Approaches to Studying questionnaire.

	Achieving	Reproducing	Meaning
End of first year	11	19	12

Students' awareness of the inadequacy of their learning will be picked up again below when we examine students' reflections on problem-based learning.

To provide a contrast, the following student described a clear deep approach:

'What I got him to do was explain exactly what was or wasn't happening—trying to get it clear—asking questions all the time...I decided that I knew how it worked and I was looking for information to reinforce that and asking questions...I asked other questions which were going to the same point but taking different loops round to it'

61

This deep approach was again confirmed by his Approaches to Studying questionnaire scores, which were markedly different to those of the student previously quoted.

	Achieving	Reproducing	Meaning
End of first year	19	8	19

These student statements highlight what the problem-based course was trying to achieve: a more active and reflective approach to learning which led to real understanding of the engineering principles involved.

The innovation

The second year Automotive Engineering Design course removed many of the causes of a surface approach. It abandoned a formal lecture programme and teacher-imposed timetable. The syllabus was greatly reduced. Exams were dropped and the assessment tasks could no longer be tackled by regurgitation. Instead the course adopted many of the strategies introduced in Chapter 2 for fostering a deep approach:

Problem-based learning

Students tackle design problems in order to generate a need to find out. The pace at which new problems are introduced depends on the level of students' understanding rather than on a fixed timetable. Lecturing is limited to that required to solve the problem and does not follow a formal schedule. The problems are so structured as to clarify learners' needs and to limit the length of formal presentations required to meet those needs.

Reflection on learning

Students keep a learning journal in which they record their reflections on learning. Tutors respond in writing to students' entries in their journals, making comments designed to encourage further, and deeper, reflection, rather than to correct or assess. Extracts from these logs are cited below as evidence of students' approach to their studying and the quality of their learning.

Students also maintain a learning log which contains a full record of the content of their learning, particularly the process of learning. Coursework is also structured to provide a period of reflection and to enable generalisations of knowledge to take place. The logs are assessed and marks contribute to the overall assessment of the year.

Independent group work

Students spend most of their time in teams throughout most of the year. Students tutor each other and co-operate on problems and projects.

Learning by doing

Students spend most of their time in a purpose-built design studio engaged in engineering design process activities. The studio has clusters of chairs around drawing boards, CAD terminals along one side and an area at one end for impromptu larger group work and lectures. Formal instruction represents a very small proportion of learning time.

Project work

Periodically throughout the year students tackle week-long projects through which they integrate and apply the knowledge and skills they have developed through group problem-based work. Towards the end of the year these projects are carried out on an individual basis.

Assessment

The assessment has also been radically changed. Instead of exams the assessment involves the learning logs, group-based tasks and individual project work, some moderated by oral examinations at which students are required to explain their design decisions. The oral assessment process is developed through informal orals used regularly as part of normal classes. The orals have proved problematic.

The introduction of a problem-based approach does not imply random learning through discovery. The curriculum involves a carefully designed matrix relating course objectives to topic areas, and carefully specified assessment criteria listing knowledge and skill areas from the curriculum. The objectives are actually specified more explicitly than on the conventional course.

The course embodies each of the four elements which foster a deep approach to a considerable extent:

Motivational context

The automotive industry which students will work in, its products and systems, form the context of the students' work. Students work primarily on problems set in this context and this is where their motivation is generated.

Learner activity

The students are continually engaged in solving real problems. There is virtually no passive learning.

Interaction with others

A substantial proportion of the work is undertaken in groups and it is not possible to tackle the problems or undertake the projects without extensive interaction. Engagement with tutors also involves more interaction as it tends to involve small group sessions rather than large group lectures.

A well structured knowledge base

The teaching approach aims to reveal and consolidate existing knowledge before introducing new material. The approach concentrates on a solid foundation of underlying concepts and understanding rather than wide coverage. The syllabus has less technical content than the parallel Mechanical Engineering course.

The following summary of a five week sequence of sessions on Solid Mechanics illustrates the way problem-based learning works in practice.

Solid Mechanics

Week 1, Day 1   *50 minute studio session*

The problem: vehicle suspension systems.
Level of students knowledge: no formal study of suspension system analysis; first year engineering science; assumed awareness of basic car design features.
The problem starts with the students being asked in groups to discuss what the purpose of a suspension system is. The lecturer assists by stimulating discussion and challenging perceptions.   (35 minutes)
In a plenary session each group is asked to contribute their conclusions and the lecturer lists significant student responses.   (15 minutes)

Week 1 Day 2   *100 minute studio session*

The study of the suspension system analysis is taken further by asking the students in their groups to discuss how the system works and how they would design it. The lecturer circulates the groups to stimulate and challenge, but not to answer or tell.   (70 minutes)
In a plenary session the groups attempt to explain how the system works. The lecturer exploits the session identify the knowledge and skills required to design a suspension system.

Week 2 Day 1   *50 minute studio session*

Introductory lecture on vector methods.   (40 minutes)
This involves a questioning session to identify any problems with the lecture material.   (10 minutes)

Week 2 Day 2   *100 minute studio session*

A practical assignment is handed out requiring the students in their groups to build with balsa wood and cotton a three-dimensional vector system. They have to measure parameters of the system and calculate the same parameters using basic trigonometry (O-level maths) comparing the two results. Finally, they are required to reflect on their experience and draw out general rules for future application.

Week 3 Day 1   *50 minute studio session*

Students are reminded of the experiential learning cycle. In their groups they are requested to continue their reflection started on Day 2 of the previous week, to generalise their new found knowledge and consider its application to the problems of the suspension system, identifying any perceived problems in its application.   (40 minutes)

They are then required to commit this to paper and share it with the group in a plenary session.   (10 minutes)

Week 3 Day 2   *100 minute studio session*

This is an interactive lecture session aimed at developing the principles of geometric modelling of three-dimensional systems, with the suspension system as the problem base. The interaction is achieved by posing problems for the groups which they should be able to solve from their observations of physical structures.   (60 minutes)
A formative assignment is introduced which applies the modelling techniques to a known suspension system and requires the students to build in balsa wood the geometric model created, checking measured dimensions against calculated ones.   (40 minutes)

Week 4 Days 1 and 2   *150 minute studio session*

The whole session is given up for the assignment set the previous week. The lecturer assists in a tutorial mode advising on methods and also on recording learning in the log book. The lecturer's solution is provided at the end of the session against which the students assess themselves.

Week 5 Day 1   *50 minute studio session*

The whole session involves interaction in which students generalise their experience from the assignment and resolve any difficulties remaining after their self-assessment.

Week 5 Day 2   *100 minute studio session*

A summative assignment is introduced on the geometric modelling of a different type of suspension. The students are each required to log all their own work, 'warts and all', and hand it in on Day 1 of week 7.

The following interaction between a student and a tutor after a similar problem-based sequence illustrates a crucial difference in the nature of student learning involved:

Student: 'Why wasn't it like this in the first year? This stress analysis is easy!'

Tutor: 'It is the same technique as it was then, wasn't it? What's the difference?'

Student: 'Yes, I suppose so, but I want to know now because I need it to design this steering system.'

Implementing the innovation

The first year this innovation ran it was undertaken with a small group. It was acknowledged that the initial investment would be high. It was necessary to involve a group of lecturers who needed to learn about the philosophy and practice of problem-based learning in order to contribute in a congruent way to the teaching of the course.

A staff development workshop was held: a five day event from 9.00 am to 9.00 pm each day. The programme was designed following an initial meeting to identify staff needs and it was attended by the entire course team. The workshop was designed in the form that staff would be expected to teach on the course. It was experiential and problem-based as well as using groups. It also required the staff to keep reflective journals which were commented on each night by the course tutor who ran the event. Each day involved a morning session concerned with the theoretical background to problem-based learning and first hand experience of problem-based methods, and the afternoons were concerned with practical applications and the development of appropriate course material. A group project lasted the whole week and was concerned with the development of a typical problem for use on the course, its management and assessment. The outcome of this group project was presented by the groups in a plenary session at the end of the week.

While the workshop had its problems it also had a major impact on some of the participants. In the evaluation one commented:

'I have been a lecturer for 25 years and this is the first time I have thought about how students learn!'.

The impact of the workshop has spread far beyond the Automotive course. Three more such workshops are being run so that all staff in the Department experience the same process. One of these workshops is specifically to introduce problem-based methods into a new Product Design course.

Once under way there was a considerable amount of shared teaching and sitting in on sessions to learn about tutoring techniques. In addition the course tutor sampled tutors' comments on students' reflective journals and collected examples of effective commenting to model tutors' behaviour.

Once it was demonstrated to work well the decision was made to expand the course to take 30 students.

Students also need to be introduced to the course. They are provided with a 30-page course guide which explains the objectives, content and rationale of the course and also the kind of learning involved. The experiential learning cycle is explained. At an early meeting with students an experiential exercise concerned with communication skills is run and analysed to demonstrate the experiential learning cycle in action. The role and importance of reflection in learning is emphasised and the use of the reflective journal explained.

Students' learning on the problem-based course

In order to interpret what happened to the quality of students' learning on the Automotive course it is helpful to first examine what happened on the Mechanical course. This is the course the students would otherwise have taken and this therefore provides the baseline against which the Automotive course can be compared. It should be remembered that at the end of the first year there were no significant differences between students on these two courses in their approaches to study or in their exam marks.

The students on the Mechanical course adopted a surface approach to a significantly greater extent at the end of the second year than at the start. They adopted a deep approach to a significantly lesser extent at the end of the second year than at the start—less even than in their first year. The quality of their learning declined. This is a phenomenon documented in other studies of undergraduates: the quality of learning can decline progressively over three years (see Chapter 1). In contrast, the students on the Automotive course adopted a surface approach to a significantly lesser extent at the end of the second year, while their deep approach remained unchanged. The difference in the way these students adopted a surface approach is illustrated in Figure 7.1.

This decline in the extent to which the Automotive students took a surface approach gives a very limited impression of the changes which took place, however. A

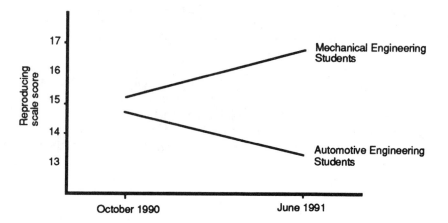

Figure 7.1: Changes in the surface approach of Mechanical and Automotive students between the start and end of the course

fuller picture emerged from the students' reflective journals, as the following extracts reveal. This first quote shows a student recognising the different demands of the course:

> 'The vagueness or open-endedness of several of the tasks so far puts more of a pressure on us working out for ourselves what to do and how to go about it. I find this difficult as I am used to being spoon-fed, ie told exactly what to do. Presumably this is one of the fundamental differences between this and other courses'.

The same student also recognised that the way he had learnt in the past was not at the same level:

> 'Solid Mechanics is one of the subjects I found interesting last year but also one that was hardest to understand. Starting off this year we have gone through stuff that I have taken for granted I knew, but actually doing it again revealed how little feel I had, even for simple details on which the new stuff is based, eg vectors, reference frames, direction cosines. This was worrying but also a good thing. If I'm worried about the gaps in my knowledge I'm likely to pay attention to such details'.

This second student had a similar experience after working out something about vectors:

> 'Having found this out for myself I looked back through my lecture notes and found proof of this conclusion that had been overlooked. I

68

was initially slightly annoyed at the fact that so much time had been wasted finding out for myself when it was in my notes all along, but on reflection this time was not wasted, since by finding out for myself I am more likely to remember this point and not get stuck on it again. After all, I had forgotten that I had written it in my notes! This experience will also teach me to read through my notes more carefully in future before tackling a problem, to prevent this from happening again.'

Students often reflected on the skills required to handle large open-ended tasks and to work co-operatively in a team and contrasted this with their previous experience. Both the new demands and reflection on them were developing the learning skills of these students, as in this example:

'We are required to work out a plan of tasks with a timescale in which to do them. To do this it is necessary to split the project into parts and estimate how long each one will take and then fit all these into the time between now and the date the project needs to be completed by. It was only when we were asked to write out a detailed list of the task left to be completed that I realised how much was involved and how much planning was necessary. Previously very little planning has been done and projects and assignments have been done in a haphazard manner. Planning a task beforehand allows more time to be spent on details without having to worry about where they fit in—as this will already have been determined.

'Another thing is interacting with design groups, working out which parts require co-operation with other members. Co-operation with other students previously had involved persuading another student to help with homework that couldn't be handled. Actually pooling ideas and learning from colleagues is new, but already it has helped, for example in the Marketing assignment which was very open-ended. Other members of the group were equally at a loss as to how to go about the assignment as I was initially, but after a short discussion we were able to form some idea about what we were collectively aiming at and also as to what each individual was going to try and do to fulfil their part.'

Students also recognised that past study habits needed changing. The following extract from a reflective journal is followed by some of the tutor's comments.

Student: '...it highlighted one of my problems that I have had for a long time—careless mistakes...I could not get the values to work out. It took me 20 minutes to find out that I hadn't square rooted to find their magnitudes. I don't feel this happened because I was distracted or not concentrating, as this kind of mistake has happened on many previous occasions. The problem perhaps lies in the speed at which I attack problems. Rushing things would perhaps cause me to miss the obvious...I have got used to rushing them. I will try in future to study the problem and the process involved more slowly and not to take it for granted the first thing that arrives in my head.'

Tutor: 'Very good reflecting ...There is a tendency to rush at things. It is developed by the exam system. Answers are needed quickly. On this course you need to develop understanding as you go along. Plan your way through, getting the concepts clear. Number crunching must be accurate, but modelling correctly is the key.'

This student reflected on the role of discussion in learning:

'The lecture was very clear with plenty of discussion on the qualities of a vector. Hence we were introduced to the triangle addition law of vectors. In the ensuing discussion which took place some of the students took a lot of persuasion that pressure has a direction but we were never fobbed off or expected just to accept the fact. About 20 minutes were spent in this discussion but I think the triangle law of addition will be remembered now. Another problem I think is that I don't contribute to discussions very often. I shouldn't be so afraid to stick my neck out and be wrong from time to time.'

The journal entries below, from three points in the year, come from a student who adopted a clear deep approach to his studies, as reflected in his scores on the Approaches to Studying questionnaire.

	Achieving	Reproducing	Meaning
October 1990	19	10	22
June 1991	19	8	19

Autumn journal entry: It is really when I sit down at home and start looking through the work that I start to really get an understanding for it.

Spring journal entry: I have clearly got to try to overcome my blind fear of maths problems and try to adopt a logical problem solving approach to it as I would for any other problem.

Summer journal entry: By giving us problems that are easy to relate to, like evaluating the performance of a Rover 800 water pump, working in groups, I have found that I have learnt quickly. I am the sort of person who finds it much easier to tackle a problem if I can relate it to something practical. I think the nature of this course is helpful to mature students because it is not just about number crunching and abstract theory. Quite a lot of emphasis is placed on practical applications of problem solving techniques which are really the most useful tools to have at your disposal in outside industry.'

The following longer extracts from the journal of one student show reflection of a high standard and highlight fascinating features of the course. This first extract contrasts the way he was encouraged to reflect on his learning with the way he was previously encouraged to pretend that there were no problems:

'The log-book is a principle I've never come across before this year. The average lecturer likes to see the right result squared in red at the bottom of the test sheet, if possible with as few lines of calculation as possible—above all, don't put any comments. He hates that. He thinks that you are trying to fill the page with words to make the work look bigger. Don't leave your mistakes either, even corrected. If you've done it wrong, bin the lot. He likes to believe that you've found the right solution at the first time. If you're still making mistakes, that means you didn't study enough. There is no way you can redo an exercise a few months after because you've only got the plain result without comments. If you have a go, you may well make the same mistakes you've done before because you've got no record of your previous errors.

The log-book is a system I really praise and used a lot. I learned to solve problems. It sounds ridiculous but one can live easily without solving one's problems. I used to avoid, to hide, the problems of understanding I could meet in class by waiting for the subject to change. In the worst case, I would fail the test and that was it. I might find the next subject easier and catch up with the results. This year, in most cases, everything was following logically... and there was no way other than understanding to proceed. This is partly due to the use of the journal... The journal helps to set the problems and to be positively critical. I found it personally very useful to express clearly ideas (which is sometimes difficult by means of words) and to keep record of it.'

The same student also contrasted the ways students used to co-operate with the ways groups now worked together:

'Group work has been another approach completely new to me. I was used to completely individual pieces of work. It doesn't mean there was no co-operation. On the contrary, students were always willing to show others the work they have done, making photocopies for you if necessary. It is efficient in terms of results but completely uninformative. You may be able to do the same exercise again but you wouldn't be capable of generalising. The amount of information you go through is enormous but completely irrelevant if you haven't understood it.

The system is the opposite of this. The amount of information is not great but you are sure you've understood everything and you are capable of using it in any situation. This year proved very useful especially methodwise. Knowing how to work in a group is also a major gift. Engineers are human beings, not only 'creation machines'. Even if I know I have to develop my group management skill to take the best of every member (individual work doesn't exist any more in industry), I have a new approach of work.'

Assessment

Assessment of all work is concerned with understanding. The following two course engineering science objectives, concerned with understanding, illustrate how far the assessment criteria have come from being concerned with knowledge alone:

- Graduates will demonstrate the ability to use the knowledge in the process of synthesising design solutions. The objective is to have developed the ability to use the knowledge intuitively in creating mechanical structures, machines and systems prior to the engineering analysis which will confirm their integrity as commercially and technically viable solutions.

- Graduates will be able to apply the knowledge accurately when analysing the technical an commercial integrity of their design proposals. They will also be able to use the analysis in developing their proposals to meet fully the objectives laid down by the design specification.

Assessment of students work was through their assignment logs. They were expected to show their complete work, 'warts and all'. They were aware that tutors were looking for understanding and that this was revealed not only in the answer they got but also in the mistakes they make, their explanation of these and their strategies for sorting them out. The following extracts from students' logs, concerned with an assignment on a trailer brake, are reproduced here together with comments from the tutor explaining why they demonstrate understanding. These are the kinds of statements in the logs which tutors are looking for in order to assess the level of students' understanding. This is clearly a very different process than that involved in much assessment in engineering.

The assignment required the students to design a mechanical system and prove that it met a specification which they had defined. They had to identify and quantify the forces applied to all the system components and to the trailer chassis. It was an individual project conducted over one week at the end of the year. The project was extended a further two weeks (part-time) due to requests from students who wished to complete the work thoroughly.

Student: 'From the first part of the analysis... it was found out that the position of the nodes was critical. It was not sufficient to measure the nodes off the drawings. It was far more accurate to calculate them.'

Tutor: 'The student here is drawing conclusions from a piece of work, comparing graphical and mathematical methods for performing the same function against criteria set by the particular circumstance of the project in hand.'

Student: 'The problem is the following—the system is not symmetrical about the axis of the trailer. Therefore, if one side is located correctly, the other will be deficient.'

Tutor: 'The student here is generalising and drawing principles from an experience which he will be able to use intuitively in future.'

Student: 'The free body is wrong. It cannot be a simple rod submitted to two forces. There is a moment on each end of it not created by these two forces.'

Tutor: 'The student here has made a hypothesis, tested it and found it wanting. On further analysis he is making a new hypothesis for how an element of his system is constrained to move which he is about to test. This is all discussed out in the open.'

Student: 'Analysis of the secondary brake operating lever will show if magnitude of force in rod to brake actuator changes at all (it shouldn't).'

Tutor: 'The "it shouldn't" indicates that the student has used his knowledge in synthesising the solution. He is now at the stage of proving his solution.'

Student: 'The only worrying aspect is the very large moment in the y—direction at point E... will need to have a very large material thickness to prevent breaking.'

Tutor: 'This demonstrates the integration in the student's mind of the analysis of forces and the design of the form and size of a component. He doesn't just leave it as a number, he attaches some significance to it which will eventually lead him to redesign to avoid the problem he perceives.'

Student: 'Most important, I have learnt the importance of taking into consideration during the initial design the method of analysis.'

Tutor: 'This quite deep statement is referring to the desire to predict with science the performance of a system. A design may be of a configuration which renders it intractable to the skill with science available to the designer or his advisors. In this sort of case it is not unusual in practice for the design to be modified, with some cost to its efficiency, to make it possible to predict performance with confidence. This reduces risk.'

Student: 'The above cannot be true. What it means is that some type of mounting is required for the compensator system since having it floating renders the system indeterminate.'

Tutor: 'Here the student has some odd results from analysis. He draw conclusions from this and links the problem to design. The analysis and synthesis are linked in the student's mind—a course objective.'

Student: 'Although the above analysis produces a correct result, it is only because the link produces no torque... to model the link correctly...'

Tutor: 'The student here has achieved what he believes to be a correct result, but is still not happy that all circumstances are covered and that he could envisage situations where his mathematical model of the design is deficient.'

Student: 'The angle doesn't have to be accurate—this is not important so long as the node changes in position are all accurate relative to each other.'

Tutor: 'Here the ability to see the critical features of his design or its model is demonstrated.'

All these comments show the sort of thinking which is demanded of the students. They all indicate understanding of the fundamentals which the assessment criteria reward.

Longer-term impacts on student learning

Several of the case studies in the project illustrate how localised, and short-lived, improvements in students' approaches to studying can be. It is not uncommon for students to revert to a dominant surface approach in parallel lecture-based courses or as soon as examinations draw close. Here the impact on students was impressively pervasive. At the end of the second year, students from both the Mechanical and Automotive courses combined to take a conventionally-taught Instrumentation course. The students who had experienced problem-based learning refused to tolerate being taught in a way which forced them to be passive, and which required them to accept the value of learning information unconnected to worthwhile problems. A parallel course has had to be designed so that the Automotive students' learning started from the vehicle, and instrumentation problems, rather than from information and theory.

In the third year, students undertake a work placement. In the fourth year students from the two courses undertake the same engineering projects. One one occasion both groups of students attended the same series of lectures and then undertook a group project assignment. The same lecturer tutored both groups. The project was concerned with the investigation of flow and aerodynamic performance of rectangular models. The students had to plan and undertake some experimental work, interpret the results of their observations and link these with theory. A report and presentation were required for assessment.

The tutor noticed a dramatic difference in the quality of learning between the two kinds of students and made the following comments:

Mechanical students:
'Ill-prepared with poor presentation and material. Technically poor. Little evidence of group working (NB. two members of one group came up with different solutions!). Only two members presented their work per group. No reports presented.'

74

Automotive students:
'Material well presented (good overheads). Each member of group said something. Technically superior to Mech. 2 out of 4 reports handed in, the rest promised by the end of the day.'

One might have expected the Automotive students to have worked better in groups, to have given better presentations and to have managed their time better—after all, these were skills they had developed through independent group project work in the second year. However, they also produced technically superior work. There was clear evidence of students having read around the subject. What is interesting is that this technical superiority came from students who had tackled a much reduced technical syllabus compared with the Mechanical students. Clearly they had learnt to tackle problems outside their experience through a sound grounding in the underlying concepts and through the use of problem-solving and learning techniques.

Costs

It is important to know whether such a problem-based course is more expensive to run than a conventional course. On the debit side it took a great deal of time to design and set up. It uses a large design studio the whole time. Assessment of the coursework and projects is time consuming and commenting on the reflective journals places a burden on the tutors who undertake this work.

On the credit side it makes far less use of the technical laboratories and no use of lecture theatres. It takes no more weekly class contact time than the Mechanical course and does not require the personal tutoring provided on the Mechanical course. In the year the case study was undertaken the Automotive course involved fewer students, but the following year it took as many students as the Mechanical course. Apart from the setting up costs it seems to cost about the same as its conventional alternatives

Conclusions

The quality of student learning has clearly changed in a marked and pervasive manner and this change has been recognised by the staff. A wide range of changes have started being introduced to encourage a deep approach in the first year of the BEng, including increasing the weighting of coursework, reducing class contact hours, introducing more investigation and application work and teaching subjects through the medium of a product design task. Staff development concerned with these methods is extending to other courses. The Institute of Mechanical Engineers has accepted the use of 100 percent course work assessment in the second year and final year. These are considerable successes after only two years of innovation. The factors which are likely to have been influential in making the innovations successful include:

- the comprehensive nature of the innovations, affecting students' entire experience in the second year rather than only one part of it;

- the staff development which engaged a significant number of staff with the underlying theory and which provided them with first hand experience of methods;

- a congruent assessment system which was focussed explicitly on rewarding understanding;

- a reduction in the size of the syllabus;

- the extent of student reflection on their learning which led to developments in their ability as learners and as members of groups;

- and, not least, the flair, energy and commitment of the innovator in seeing through a radical departure from previous practice in the Department.

Chapter 8

Encouraging reflection and independence on a Graphic Information Design course

Allan Davies, Falmouth School of Art and Design

This case study describes a range of related innovations designed to increase students' reflectiveness, independence and interdependence. Design courses traditionally involve extensive project work. The course studied here also used co-operative group work, increased discussion and reflection, and involvement of the students in their assessment. The case study describes significant changes in the ways students approach their learning.

The context

This case study concerns a four-year BA Graphic Information Design sandwich course. It differs from general graphic design courses in that it is concerned with visual communication of information, in the sense of reducing uncertainty, as a priority over persuasive or stylistic concerns. It emphasises the needs of the user of the graphic information and recognises the need for theoretical understanding and for collaboration with specialists in the information being communicated. Students go on to employment in situations such as publishing, specialist design groups, computer graphics and audio/visual companies.

A range of innovations had been introduced over the three years before the case study was undertaken and these innovations form an important backdrop because they were, to an extent, conceived within the same overall theoretical framework as the Improving Student Learning project.

Due to the nature of design education the 'Approaches to Studying' questionnaire was not a suitable device for measuring students' approach to learning as the questions refer to essays, reading, and having to memorise facts in a way which is largely inappropriate. Nevertheless, the questionnaire was used to compare the first and fourth years of the course to see if the range of innovations introduced had an impact over the span of the whole course. As the innovations of concern here were introduced gradually there was no opportunity for clear before-and-after comparisons. Also the other courses at the School, such as those involving Fine Art, were too dissimilar for realistic comparisons between courses to be made. As a consequence what follows is largely descriptive, supported with interview data where appropriate.

Earlier innovations

Innovations began as a response to declining staff resources but were then recognised as of educational value and extended. The innovations had two broad aims:

- increasing student independence;
- increasing group effectiveness and student interdependence.

The intention was to increase students' active involvement in the learning process. Many of the innovations were, while new to the staff concerned, not new to design education, and many involved fine tuning of methods rather than radical course re-design.

Objectives and criteria

Underlying the individual innovations, however, was a rethinking of the course objectives and criteria for assessment. The criteria were particularly interesting because they relate directly to Säljö'scategories of description of levels of sophistication of students' conception of learning. The assessment criteria were divided into eight 'domains' in the following way:

A The conceptual

    1. Ideas

    2. Information

B The productive

    1. Information design

    2. Materials

    3. Media

C The contextual/critical

D Lifeskills

1. Personal skills

2. Interpersonal skills

For each of these domains four levels of achievement were specified, from a basic competence to a mature competence, in order to clarify for students what each grade means and what they need to do in order to improve their grades. The description of these levels is shown in Table 8.1.

Surface learning is essentially learning by rote. It depends on memory rather than understanding and it can only be reapplied in a situation identical to the one initially encountered. Surface learning does not last. Deep learning, on the other hand, leads to understanding, to the ability to determine inter-relationships and to apply underlying principles. This implies a capacity to transfer thinking and performance to other situations. Deep learning is long-lasting.

These assessment descriptions should form the basis of the self-, peer-, and tutor-assessment programme.

Level 1   This is learning that students perceive is done to them by teachers rather than something they do. Learning is memorising. The student has an active role in memorising, but the information being memorised is not transformed in any way.

Level 2   This is learning that is acquiring facts, skills or procedures which are to be used. What is learned is seen as needed in order to do things as a later date, but there is still no transformation of what is learnt by the learner.

Level 3   This is learning that makes sense. The student makes active attempts to abstract meaning in the process of learning.

Level 4   This is learning as understanding reality. Learning enables the student to perceive the world differently. The student sees her work in a world context and recognises its value.

Table 8.1: Levels of achievement for assessment criteria domains

Achievements in each of the eight domains were then described at each of the four levels in order to clarify assessment criteria. The first of these four levels of achievement corresponds to Säljö'slevels 1 and 2 and levels 2–4 correspond to Säljö'slevels 3–5 (Table 8.1). This is a rare example of an attempt to produce a general set of criteria concerning quality in learning, rather than content, and which have meaning for all learning, regardless of subject matter.

Assessment profiles

The criteria used to assess students' work and projects have not always been clear in design education. In this course a system was introduced involving the use of an 'assessment profile'. This is a sheet containing space to list the items being submitted for assessment and a space for listing five assessment criteria with a five-point rating scale against each criterion. Initially the tutors specified the criteria and made the ratings from which marks were derived. This succeeded in clarifying the goals of projects but did little to involve students. The next steps have involved student discussion and negotiation of criteria, student self-assessment using the criteria and ratings prior to submitting the work, and even negotiation of grades. In this way students have become more involved in decision making about the learning they undertake and have developed their judgment about criteria and standards.

Crits

The 'crit' is an established component of nearly all art, design and architecture courses. It involves the presentation of a collection of visual work to a group—often a large group including the tutors. Major crits can involve an entire year group. Students commonly perceive these crits as intimidating and they are often dominated by a few vociferous students and staff.

> '...it did really frighten some people. It wasn't confidence building to make them go up there and do it, it was just making them worse.'

> 'The group crits were a bit like trial by jury, you had to stand up and defend your work against a big lot of people who could well be attacking it.'

> '...those were kind of scary and you were actually afraid to stand up in front of the year. It was terrifying to explain your work, terrified of the outcome...'

> 'Some people deliberately cut themselves off...they were put off by the crits in the first year, that can do somebody's confidence no good.'

Crits occur at the end of a project, but for many this is unhelpful:

> 'It was all too late. If you were going to make mistakes then you had made them and they showed up in your final work, then you were on to another project and you can't go back and rectify them or sort them out properly.'

> '...all we had was a crit at the end of it so by that time it was too late to change and you were stuck there with that piece of work. People would give you advice then but then it would be too late.'

80

In large groups the process could become repetitive and student involvement could be very low.

'It was all right if you were the first person in the group ... but by the time you got to number 30 everyone was falling asleep and by the time you had got to the eighth piece of work anyway everything that was going to be said about nearly all the work had already been said and the tutor was just repeating himself.'

In order to reduce anxiety, which lowers the quality of learning, and increase productive interaction, two changes were made. First, the size of group at crits was reduced. Second, groups were helped to reflect on what went wrong at crits and to develop group behaviour which supported learning more effectively. In the first year, students sometimes ran their own crits without staff present. In the second year students undertook more advanced analysis of their group processes, aided by a psychologist, and developed ways of handling their crits which worked better. Staff have had to ask permission to attend! These crits were sometimes based on their tutorial groups.

Student-initiated briefs

Traditionally the dominant method of teaching design, particularly on graphics-focussed courses, has been that of a brief being written by the tutor to be acted upon by the student. The method simulated, to some extent, the professional practice of designers but it also perpetuated the power relationship between tutor and student. Furthermore an important characteristic of information design is that the information designer does not simply receive briefs, but identifies information problems. Information designers are proactive about problems rather than simply reactive to briefs. As a consequence the final year major design requires students to identify and act upon what they feel to be genuine information design problems. They are responsible for writing their own briefs and this is an important part of the whole project.

Tutorial groups

This innovation is the one which has been studied as part of the Improving Student Learning project.

Design work is often a solitary business and this can be reflected in the quality of work presented at the end of projects which may reveal little reflection and little consideration of alternatives to the designs produced. The only discussion students get involved in had tended to be with tutors. Individual tutorials were becoming harder to resource and also tended to be dominated by the tutor. There had been a series of initiatives to increase the amount of interaction between students so as to foster reflection.

In the final year the largest component of students' work and assessment involved independent work, including a major project. After a project brief had been agreed the student was allocated a tutor. It was the students' responsibility to arrange contact with the tutor as they felt necessary. Other tutors with specialist knowledge could be consulted by arrangement. This had been the only tutorial support the students received and there were no opportunities for students to interact together in an organised way except for the crits on completion of the projects when assessment took place.

Strongly motivated and well organised students tended to survive this situation with reasonable success. Others did not fare so well. While the emphasis on individual responsibility was still considered appropriate, a number of problems were identified:

- Tutorial support for students was often insufficient if the student did not, for whatever reasons, seek to organise it.

- Tutorial advice, when given, often took the form of handing over knowledge from tutor to student. Students would tend to approach tutors for answers and adopt a passive approach to learning.

- There was no opportunity to compare, contrast and debate differing views on project work or to extend thinking into broader design issues.

- There were no opportunities to involve students in learning from their peers or helping their peers to learn.

As a reaction to this situation in the final year tutorial groups were established and required to meet once a week with their tutor in 90-minute sessions. The groups would be about eight in number: large enough to extend debate and vary views, but not so large that they became threatening. Although a tutor was allocated to each group it was stressed that their role would not be dominant and that the students would have to manage their own meetings.

It is important to recognise that in conventional group tutorial sessions all the students would be at the same stage and probably studying the same material to a teacher-imposed timetable. Here each student would be undertaking a unique project to their own schedule. This is therefore a method applicable to any substantial project or dissertation work which would previously have been undertaken by students in isolation from each other, but which could instead bring students together to discuss their parallel independent work.

No constraints were placed on the operation and aims of the meetings which students determined for themselves. Ground rules for the operation of the groups were often discussed and made explicit. For example:

- No member, including the tutor, should interrupt another.

- The tutor will not break silences.

- Attendance and punctuality are responsibilities that each member has to the whole group.

As these groups developed they became more autonomous and students started giving presentations to each other without the tutor being present. These sessions operated successfully entirely independently of staff.

The study

Depth interviews were conducted with students in which their approach to their studies and the reactions to their previous experiences and the tutorial groups were explored. What follows are extracts from these interviews, selected to illustrate the main themes which emerged.

In this first extract a student explains what she learnt from her unstructured tutorial group when students brought work in to be discussed.

> Student: 'What I have learnt about my work really (is) it's very easy to become so blinkered that you lose a general overview of it. You can't really see the wood for the trees. You're too close to your work, and letting other people have a look and point out the most obvious glaring things is always of value. I also think in the real world you get a lot less chances to let people to have a quick look at your work. I think you get the job you do to a certain level, you show it to the client and they tell you what they like and what they don't and then you go back and do it again. You don't really chat about it and crit it and I enjoy that kind of criticism because I do make a lot of mistakes. I think the tutorials are really valuable.'

> Interviewer: 'What can you do in a tutorial then that you couldn't achieve with group crits? What does it enable you to do?'
> Student: 'Talk... people don't have the courage to speak out and say something... people are more relaxed and you get a bit nearer the truth.'

Students also recognised the way the tutorials increased their responsibility as learners:

> Interviewer: 'Since participating in the tutorial scheme how do you think your approach to learning has changed?'
> Student: 'Well I think I realised the need for a greater responsibility as a designer and as a member of the group in terms of I am responsible for whatever I offer to the group and also responsible to them to make the group function better.'

The groups had an impact on how reflective and rigorous students were in relation to their design work.

> Interviewer: 'How do you think your learning has changed because of your involvement in the group?'
> Student: 'I am more attentive to... looking more objectively at my work

because I know that somebody else is going to look at it...sometimes it's not pleasant to find out very objective things about the work, things that you did not see...but you learn more in the long run.'

And:

Interviewer: 'Do you think it has developed your capacity to look critically at other people's work without dismissing it out of hand?'
Student: 'Yes, you can see the good points. You can look at something and think it's diabolical but there again you will look closer and pick out the better points and maybe advise them. That's nice, that works well there ...'
Interviewer: 'So it's enabled your critical capacity then?'
Student: 'Yes, definitely. I would have said that it was obvious that it had. If I look at someone's work long enough, I can pick out something, even if it looks dreadful from the outside, or if it looks brilliant you can pick out something that is not quite right. Outward appearances may look fantastic but it might not work as a information device.'

Criticism seems to have been both more pointed and more acceptable in the tutorial groups.

'Somebody will say to you "I don't like the way you have done that, because I can't read it". People don't have any qualms about saying things like that. That really helps.'

Students also contrasted the intimacy and informality of the tutorials with the crits, and the way it allowed for criticism to be productive rather than destructive:

'...now it's much easier to sit down once a week and show something in progress, get the advice off them, it's so much easier.'

'It needed to be a more efficient kind of critique where the people you were with actually knew the work that you were doing and were more acquainted with you. I like the kind of intimacy, I like the potential for very critical feedback and response in a kind of environment where everybody knows each other... it's a chance to be more intimate ...'

'...these groups have really helped because you know the individuals now. There is trust in the fact that you will get some feedback.'

Students gained a great deal from each other and the tutor was not always felt to be necessary:

'I can take something into a tutorial and say "I haven't really got a clue how to do this", and your tutor may not necessarily have really good advice on how to do it, but the other students will because they have faced the same problem, real production methods ...'

'I have been the kind of person who really did get in with three or four people and we did discuss our work, we went to each other's houses ...worked in small groups with my colleagues.'

This interdependence was not just helpful, but absolutely necessary if the students were to cope with the degree of independence the later years of the course required:

Interviewer: 'The third year represents a move from tutor-led to student-led where you have full responsibility. Do you think that the tutorials help?'
Student: 'Yes. They do. I find it hard to imagine what it would be like without the tutorials, actually. I've already mentioned keeping going from one week to the next—you've got to have that motivation ... there is nobody standing there saying "why isn't this done" or "your deadline's not been met" and (the tutorials) give you an incentive to keep going. I find them particularly helpful at the moment because the tutor's aren't coming round to see us so it's down to us ... so its nice to have a situation where I can ask people.'

There was clearly a considerable degree of personal development going on as students learnt to work with others in the tutorials, and again this was contrasted with attitudes and behaviour in the crits:

Interviewer: 'What kinds of skills do you think you are picking up?'
Student: 'Diplomacy! You can't just sit there and tell someone "that's crap!" You have to say, maybe there would be a better way... because you have to speak to different people in a different manner. You have to look at the person you are speaking to and it's getting to know people... In crits ... it comes out "yours is rubbish" that kind of thing, "did you hear what he said about your work, ha!" that kind of thing. I certainly wasn't willing to go into tutorials when we first had them and speak about the work because I was not happy with it.'

'...you gain confidence and you also become more relaxed with people.'

'...we have been addressing fundamental problems that affect the groups that I have been in ...because we have had problems getting the group going... so we have been dealing with those, trying to make them function more effectively.'

The Approaches to Studying questionnaire was administered in the middle of the year to the first year students and also to fourth year students, to see if the range of measures introduced had an impact on students' approaches to studying over the four years of the course (see Table 8.2).

Two points are worthy of note here. First, it might be assumed that students on Design courses would automatically take a deep approach and that a surface approach

Middle of first year (n = 34)	15.24	12.35	15.03
Middle of fourth year (n = 23)	14.13	9.70	18.35

Table 8.2: Mean scores on the Approaches to Studying questionnaire

would be entirely missing, especially in the first year, where students are often given very open exploratory work to undertake. However, while the scores in the first year indicate that students take a deep approach to a greater extent than a surface approach, the scores are not so very different from those in some of the other case studies of conventional academic courses. As illustrated in some of the quotes above, it is possible to take a surface approach to design work and an extensive deep approach cannot be taken for granted.

Second, there is evidence (see Chapter 1) that students adopt a surface approach to a progressively greater extent, and a deep approach to a declining extent, as they progress through higher education. Some of the other case studies also found this decline in the quality of learning amongst students on conventional courses running parallel to that being studied. Here, in contrast, there was a significant decline in the extent of a surface approach ($p < 0.01$) to an unusually low mean Reproducing score and also a significant increase in the extent of a deep approach ($p < 0.001$). There was no significant change in the Achieving score. While there is no control group here, and this data compares two different student groups rather than following one group through the four years, overall the range of steps taken to foster a deep approach appear to have been particularly successful.

Key features and conclusions

The innovations which have produced the effects described above by the students embody the following key features which foster a deep approach.

- Allowing students to choose their own information design problem and write their own brief enhanced the motivational context of their final year work. Students were working on a problem which mattered to them which they were motivated to tackle.

- The design work involved activity—though this was not a new feature. Previously, however, the potential of the practical activity had not been fully realised.

- The tutorial groups fostered interaction, both within and outside the regular meetings. Students joined in more and discussed their work more openly and much more frequently.

- The way students regularly encountered different perspectives and views helped them to construct a wider and better balanced knowledge base.

The strategies which embody these features which the course used included:

- independent learning, always present but now involving a greater element of student decision making;

- personal development, supported by the trust and intimacy of the tutorial groups and also challenged by the demands of working in such groups;

- a problem focus, inherent in information design, but now emphasised through students' identification of their own problem and specification of their own brief instead of responding passively to a given brief;

- increased reflection, brought about by the tutorial groups;

- independent group work, as the tutors were able to withdraw and the tutorial groups started meeting on their own;

- learning by doing, always a strong element of the course;

- the development of learning skills, here emphasising learning how to learn in groups;

- fine-tuning, illustrated in the specification of assessment criteria for projects and the continuing efforts to help students to make their groups work effectively. Without continuing assistance it is common for such group work to fail through lack of students' group skills.

Although this case study involved incremental development from a form of course design which traditionally involves many features which foster a deep approach, it demonstrates the substantial scope which can exist for further development and fine tuning without disruption of a well established pattern. In particular it highlights the potential benefits of organised group work in what is traditionally an individualistic pursuit.

Chapter 9

Active and passive learning in Management Accounting

Innovator: David Lane, Portsmouth Polytechnic

This case study is an account of a failed innovation. An attempt to improve the quality of student learning in a final year Accounting course through active learning in lectures had to be abandoned. A good deal can be learnt from the reasons for this failure.

Context

The focus of the study was a compulsory final year Management Accounting course, part of a four year degree in Accounting. The course was taken by all 70 Accounting students and also 30 students from a BA Business Studies. The Accounting degree had a conventional pattern of course delivery and assessment, involving lectures and seminars and assessment primarily by three hour unseen exams. Management Accounting involved one lecture, and one seminar in a group of 12, each week for two terms. Assessment was by two pieces of coursework and a three hour unseen exam. The course was taught by the innovator, David Lane, and a colleague. They divided the course up into topic areas and took turns to teach for three or four weeks on their topics. The seminar groups were shared between David Lane, the colleague, and a third tutor who took the seminar groups of Business Studies students.

Despite being in the final year of a degree programme the students took a predominantly surface approach to their studies. Table 9.1 shows that the surface approach scores of students was higher than their deep approach scores and higher than social science norms, at the start of the Management Accounting course. This was not a consequence of the demands of the Management Accounting course alone—a final year Economics course revealed similarly high surface approach scores and lower deep approach scores. This is an indication that the Business School as a whole may be fostering a surface approach.

	Achieving	Reproducing	Meaning
Management Accounting (n = 46)	14.74	15.63	14.48
Economics (n = 43)	13.47	15.23	13.23
Social Science norms	12.73	13.65	14.21

Table 9.1: Mean scores on the Approaches To Studying questionnaire at the start of the final year

These students' motivation was not in question: their 'Achieving' scores were relatively high, though we shall see what kind of motivation this was. The impression given by the questionnaire data was confirmed in interviews. These extracts from interviews are accompanied by the student's scores on the Approaches to Studying questionnaire.

'I'm basically note-taking—putting this into lists. I'm not trying to understand in depth, to understand every move from basic principles...I have a good short-term memory, I can memorise enough to get through the exam. I don't expect to learn anything from lectures—it's just getting across information. If you regurgitate the lectures you should be able to get a bottom 2:1...I'm sticking to standards and rules.'

Achieving	Reproducing	Meaning
8	16	5

'I'm trying to absorb as much as I can, to take in information to get through the exam.'

Achieving	Reproducing	Meaning
11	16	6

Interviewer: 'what do you mean by "learning"?'

Student: 'It's gaining knowledge ... applying to practical problems ... some lecturers are like school teachers. They want you to learn what they're trying to teach.'

Achieving	Reproducing	Meaning
9	18	8

These are fairly extreme patterns of scores. They reveal extrinsic motivation and a certain cynicism about learning as well as a dominant surface approach and unusually low 'Meaning' scores.

The problem

The above data would provide a clear definition of a problem of almost whatever one was trying to teach. In the context of Management Accounting it was particularly worrying because students will encounter very varied accounting practices in business and will need to be flexible problem-solvers rather than simply employing the traditional methods and algorithms they have memorised for exams.

The innovation

It was not possible to reach any agreement on overall changes to the Management Accounting course. The innovator's colleague did not agree to change any aspect of his own teaching or to change the assessment in any way, even to the modest proposal of changing the exam to an open-book exam. It was, therefore, decided to attempt to influence students' approach to learning through the introduction of active learning into the lectures and to support this move with more open-ended exam questions for those parts of the course the innovator taught.

Active learning in lectures is also the theme of the case study in Chapter 6, although here the form the sessions took was rather different. There was a deliberate attempt to force students to take more responsibility for their own learning by employing extended open-ended, problem-based tasks even in a banked lecture theatre with 100 students present. Characteristically students would be asked to form groups and would be handed a copy of a problem for them to tackle, such as the one reproduced in Table 9.2. The problems were typically open-ended and required considerable thought as to the best approach. They could not be tackled on the basis of memorised algorithms. Students were asked to read from a text book before the session to provide them with ideas and methods for tackling the problems.

A neutral observer sat in on two of these sessions in the Spring term, the first of which involved students working on the above problem. Students had been set a chapter to read from a text book in advance. By this time in the year attendance had already dropped off sharply—an issue discussed below in the context of students' evaluations of the course.

The session began with an introduction explaining that traditional methods for calculating the percentage of defective goods were being replaced and that the more up-to-date methods were in the text book. The overall theory was briefly summarised. The reading for the following week was set, and then students were given the problem

Problem: Computing the Percentage of Defective Items

The Juran Company has a simple production process for its basic product. Two metal sections are fabricated in separate production processes and are joined together in an assembly operation. Each of the two production processes produces, on average, 5% defective items and the assembly process also operates with a 5% defect rate. To prevent bad items from being shipped to customers, inspection is done only after the assembly process.

1. What defect rate will be noted in the inspection process?

2. How much will the percentage of defects found during inspection drop if the production and assembly processes improve from 95% good parts to 99% good parts?

3. Another product of the Juran Company goes through ten consecutive processing stages. What must be the yield of good items from each stage if the company wants to have a failure rate below 1% of items going through the final inspection? What parts-per-million (PPM) defect rate does this correspond to for each stage?

Table 9.2: A typical problem for students

and asked to work on it in small groups. They formed twos, threes and fours. This introduction took about 15 minutes.

For the next 10 minutes students were observed to be thoroughly engaged in the task. The observer reported:

> 'My impression was that students were puzzling over the questions and discussing them. It was also clear that some students did not have a clue how to do it. David's rapport with students was friendly and egalitarian. The quality of debate was high and the level of involvement great. David spent a good deal of time with one student and one group. I felt that some of the others at the front might have been feeling a little neglected. They were still trying to sort out the question and discussing it, however. There was no evidence students were discussing anything else or engaging in idle chit-chat.'

The banked lecture theatre was clearly unsuitable for this kind of work and prevented access to some groups and prevented them from asking questions.

After 25 minutes on the problem students were presented with an explanation of the answers. The observer commented:

> 'I have no doubt that this method encourages deep approaches—in the way that it gets students to dialogue with the ideas. The level of discussion and interest was high.'

The second session which was observed started on a similar way. Students were asked to get into groups of five. The observer reported:

> 'They appeared not to know how to do this. . . getting into fives was a real struggle. David directed minimally. I felt there was a whole interpersonal dimension which had been missed out in these students' education. They were in the final year of their degree and unable to get themselves quickly and efficiently into groups. The tiered lecture room didn't help. But the students did not seem to have the concept of working in anything other than rows.'

The first problem was not well understood. After 20 minutes, a role play exercise was introduced. Students clearly did get on with performing this role play. The links between it and Management Accounting were not clear enough to them and there were no clear role briefs to help them. They were inexperienced in undertaking role plays and again the lecture theatre was far from ideal for this kind of work. Some students started leaving and then others followed. A useful discussion continued with the 12 students who remained.

The observer made the following overall comments on the classroom methods used:

- 'The physical space used for the sessions—a 150–seat lecture theatre—was quite inappropriate for this kind of work.

- The lecture theatre also gave messages about the nature of knowledge and the teaching process which went against what David was trying to convey. It also reinforced the authority structure/hierarchy of student and teacher, and encouraged paternalism and dependency.

- It was clear that the students were not used to group work. David's assumptions that they were autonomous individuals was made against a culture of dependency which appears to have been their previous experience.

- (The method) clearly disorients students when they do not know how to respond. They are thrown on their own resources which, it could be argued, facilitates the development of autonomy. The problem is they have only a one-hour session. This may not be enough to seriously develop the students as autonomous learners.'

Evaluation and changes

Though some students liked the methods used, many were outraged. Attendance dropped considerably. Student ratings of these sessions (on a five–point rating scale where 1 = well below average benefit and 5 = well above average benefit) were very poor, averaging 2.4. Students commented:

'I don't think I've learnt a single thing in the workshop-style lectures'

'The experimental lectures were rubbish with no benefit. Would still prefer to have proper full lectures.'

'He did not lecture to us—lecture used as a seminar but we have not covered the subject therefore no lecture notes to revise from.' (from a student with a high surface and low deep approach)

A student deputation to the course leader led to the innovator being instructed by the Head of Department to abandon the innovation. A compromise was reached in which the sessions would contain a lecture for the first half, followed by a problem session in groups.

Student ratings improved (to 2.9) and more students started recognising something of worth in the approach.

'Dave's not as bad as everyone makes out. If you are used to it you can follow it. Just lately he has been excellent' (This student gained a First Class Honours degree).

'Theoretically speaking he is correct in that most people blindly copy down the OHPs and do not understand what they are writing down.'

'D.L's modified lecture style is good. He's not as bad as everyone makes out. He makes you think about what you are doing rather than mindlessly writing it down.'

Students also criticised other conventional lectures:

'Lecturers say they want your opinions but in fact you have to conform to their opinions or else you don't do well. Lectures produce stereotyped students. I don't like having to take notes in lectures. I would prefer to concentrate on understanding.'

Others pointed to problems in the way the active learning methods were used:

'He needs to communicate better with us. His style is very new to us and he must let us know what he expects us to do for them, eg read ahead.'

'I don't think the lecture is the correct place for role play.'

The following quotes illustrate students taking a deep approach to the course, together with their scores on the Approaches to Studying questionnaire:

Achieving	Reproducing	Meaning
14	7	22

'Learning is about understanding—an increased understanding has made me feel more confident. As an Accountant you work things out as you go along based on your understanding—you don't need to remember so much.'

Interviewer: 'What are you trying to do when you learn?'

Student: 'I don't learn anything unless I understand the reason behind it'

Interviewer: 'What makes a person a competent accountant?'

Student: 'The ability to use information in a structured manner and the ability to come up with alternative methods. You don't take everything at face value.'

Achieving	Reproducing	Meaning
20	9	18

Interviewer: 'What are you trying to do when you learn?'

	Achieving		Reproducing		Meaning	
	Start	End	Start	End	Start	End
Management Accounting (n = 46, start; 46,end)	14.74	14.93	15.63	13.30	14.48	13.85
Economics (n = 43, start; 35, end)	13.47	14.29	15.23	14.77	13.23	13.40

Table 9.3: Mean scores on the Approaches to Studying questionnaire for Management Accounting and Economics students at the start and end of the final year

Student: 'I try to fully understand and to make sense of it...relate it to other subjects and decide whether its important and why'

Achieving	Reproducing	Meaning
17	11	21

These statements from students, and their scores, are dramatically different from the students described above taking a surface approach at the start of the course. The course seemed to contain two very distinct types of students. Those who did not like the active learning in lectures stopped coming. When the Approaches to Studying questionnaire was administered for a second time, towards the end of the course, many of these students had stopped attending. In fact these students took a surface approach to a significantly greater extent than those who continued to attend ($p < .01$). The extent to which a surface approach was adopted declined significantly ($p < .001$), while on the parallel Economics course there was no such decline in surface approaches, as shown in Table 9.3.

Apart from the decline in the Reproducing scores of students on the Management Accounting course, no other changes were statistically significant.

Seminars

The seminars which the innovator ran involved giving students, a week beforehand, a problem to undertake in preparation. In the main students did work on these problems during the week. The seminars themselves started with an open invitation to discuss anything of significance to the students: 'What shall we do today?'. Students tended to raise questions related to lectures or assignments which led into useful discussion. The group, usually of about 12, then split into sub-groups of three or four and attempted to arrive a a group answer to the problems. Each group then presented their solutions in a plenary session. Except where there were numerical problems there was no 'right answers' and so these presentations led to further discussion. It had been assumed that this kind of interactive problem-solving process was also operating in the parallel seminars run by the other two tutors involved, until on one occasion the innovator took one of these other seminar groups in order to cover for the colleague. The introductory: 'What shall we do today?' was met with silence. When the question was re-phrased there was still no response. Eventually the students were asked what normally happened in their seminars and they reported that the other tutor used them as further opportunities to give lectures and present model answers to the problems. It appeared that even the seminars were passive experiences elsewhere on the course.

Assessment

There were two pieces of assessed coursework in the course: one set by each of the two main tutors. The normal assignment type had been caricatured by the innovator as: 'Tell me everything there is to know about X'. Instead, he set a task involving a brief case study and open-ended questions requiring understanding and analysis. The case study included a description of the setting involving the financial performance of a hospital laundry department and a copy of a memo containing financial data. The questions required students to:

a) 'discuss in detail the various possible effects on the behaviour of the laundry supervisor of the way the budget was prepared and the form and content of the performance report, having in mind the published research findings in this area;

b) re-draft, giving explanations, the performance report and supporting memorandum in a way which, in your opinion, would make them more effective management tools.'

This assignment succeeded in producing some excellent answers, but many still consisted largely of pages of regurgitated extracts from all the literature regardless of its relevance to the case. Students were so used to producing this kind of material for assignments that they continued to do so even when it was quite inappropriate.

The other coursework assignment remained unchanged.

The exam paper consisted of eight questions, four set by the innovator and four by the colleague. The four which related to the classes involving active learning were open-ended in nature, eg:

a) What is meant by the term 'agency theory'? (5 marks)

b) Construct a numerical example which illustrates the application of agency theory in a management accounting

context. (20 marks)

In contrast, the four questions set by the colleague were all numerical problems of a similar form to those presented in lectures and worked on in seminars and capable of being tackled through the memorisation of an algorithm.

	(Meaning−Reproducing) scores	
	Top 10 students	Bottom 10 students
'Open' exam questions	12.75	11.25
Numerical questions	12.57	13.10

Table 9.4: Examination marks on open and numerical questions of students taking a deep or surface approach

Students who took a surface approach chose to tackle the numerical questions rather than the open questions and fewer students, overall, chose to tackle the open questions, as one would have predicted given students' approach to the course.

A comparison was made to see whether students who took a predominantly surface or deep approach performed differently with these types of questions. Students' 'Reproducing' scores were subtracted from their 'Meaning' scores, to give a single index of their approach. The students with the highest ten and lowest ten scores on this index were then compared (Table 9.4), ie the students with the most extreme deep or surface approaches. The marks in this Table were out of 25.

As can be seen, on the open exam questions students taking a deep approach did better than those taking a surface approach (an average of six percent better), while on the numerical questions those taking a surface approach did better. Students who took a surface approach scored seven percent less on the open questions than on the numerical questions whereas students who took a deep approach did not differ on the two types of question.

This is a clear demonstration of the different demands made by these two types of assessment demand. Given the contradictory demands in the two halves of the course it is not surprising that there was no significant correlation between overall exam marks and either Reproducing or Meaning scores.

An attempt was made to explore the relationship between the quality of students' exam answers, as measured using the SOLO taxonomy, and the approach students took to their studies. No distinct patterns were apparent for either the open or the numerical questions on the Management Accounting course, or on the parallel Economics course.

Conclusions

The innovator was removed from the course after this innovation. It was suggested that he should be kept away from both final year and first year students because the final and first years were 'too important to experiment with'. As an attempt to improve student learning it was largely ineffective, though some students benefited and a surface approach was less prevalent by the end. As an attempt to introduce new techniques into the Department it was a disaster, although the innovator was invited to run a staff development event on student-centred learning! Here was a situation with a clear problem in terms of the quality of student learning and where the methods introduced in an attempt to improve the situation have been demonstrated to have positive impacts in other contexts. What went wrong?

The following observations are offered both as an analysis of what happened, and also as advice to potential innovators in similarly constrained contexts. This advice is pursued further in Chapter 14.

- The context here was uniform and well established. Students had experienced one way of learning for the previous two years and expected to continue in that way. None of their other final year courses made unconventional demands on them. It was perhaps expecting too much that one course could achieve much in such a context.

- Only limited parts of the course could be changed—half the lectures and less than half the seminars. It was possible for students to ignore those parts of the course involving the innovations and many did just that. Even for those parts of the course which students did not ignore they were being given two quite contradictory messages about what kind of learning was required.

- The assessment was largely unchanged. One of the two coursework assignments was unchanged and the exam was unchanged in format. On the exam half the questions were unchanged in the nature of their demands, and most students chose these conventional questions. The assessment system is the most powerful lever available to influence students and here this lever was not available.

- No other staff were involved with, or even sympathetic to, the innovation, not even the colleague with whom the course was shared. As soon as things started to go wrong colleagues immediately stamped on the innovation rather than looking for ways to make it work. It is extremely difficult to make any innovation work without allies.

- Students as unused as these were to active learning, learning in groups and taking responsibility for their own learning, are likely to need more than could be offered in one-hour lecture slots to change them and to develop their abilities as learners. Most lacked the skill and sophistication as learners to cope and nothing was offered to help them to develop.

- A large banked lecture theatre is not a suitable environment for such teaching. Some methods, such as role play, are likely to fail in such a room even with co-operative students and an experienced lecturer. However it is possible to use active learning methods effectively in such a room (see Chapter 6).

- With a large class of students unused to working in this way it is necessary to start gently and to use plenty of structure to sessions. It is necessary to explain thoroughly why methods are being used, to make requirements (such as reading in advance) very clear, and to introduce innovations in a way which carries students with you. Here many students were alienated early on.

The response of students and staff is interesting here. Students complained because they were not getting what they were used to. The feedback ratings were very poor. However such ratings need to be interpreted with care. As discussed in Chapter 1, what students think good teaching consists of depends on their conception of learning. Many of these students appeared to have an unsophisticated conception of learning and the 'closed' conception of teaching which goes with it. When confronted with more 'open' teaching, they considered it 'bad' teaching. Other staff were quick to respond to students' reactions, however unsophisticated they might have been. There seems to have been scope here for everyone involved to explore further what quality in learning really consists of.

Chapter 10

Independent group fieldwork in Oceanography

Innovator: Geoff Millward, Plymouth Polytechnic South West

This case study is concerned with a field-based practical course involving oceanographic and hydrographic survey work. Changes involved introducing group work, more independence, the development of various transferable skills and an open-ended simulation element to replace routine practicals. The changes had a marked effect on students' approaches to studying and on the quality of student learning outcomes. However, the pressure of other conventional course demands limited the success of the innovation.

Context

The programmes of which the course studied here are a part were a BSc Marine Studies and a post-graduate Diploma Hydrosurvey. Both courses have a specific vocational orientation. Decision-making on major capital projects concerning the shelf seas around the British Isles, such as oil exploration, pipelining, undersea mining, wave power abstraction, outfall location, fish farming and coastal defences, and the effective control of water pollution, is based on the acquisition and interpretation of marine environmental data. The task of carrying out these tasks lies with marine institutes and consultancies. Contact with these organisations over the recent past has identified deficiencies in undergraduate and postgraduate training in key professional skills. Many employers found themselves having to spend time and money training graduates in basic skills that should have been acquired as a component of undergraduate courses. These included fieldwork skills, data handling and communication skills, especially in the written form. One employer reported:

'We find it astonishing that many graduates cannot understand the significance of results they obtain from environmental surveys. We have to put senior oceanographers onto the interpretation of some of the most straight-forward data and this puts us under man-power pressure, especially since we expect the recent graduates to be equipped for these simple tasks.'

Graduates who are in employment in the field have also voiced criticisms. For example a Marine Studies Graduate from 1989, now at the Proudman Oceanographic Laboratory wrote:

'Fewer modules on the degree would have enabled a deeper knowledge in specific areas ... a deeper understanding of the physical processes of oceanography would enable me to appreciate the work I am involved in more fully'.

This graduate also criticised the lack of depth of computing studies. A lack of depth was apparent in many comments from students about their studies on the Marine Studies course. It was clear from interviews that a significant number of students wanted to take a deep approach. Unfortunately, the system did not encourage them to do it. Typical statements included:

'I try to understand but it is much easier to try to remember... memorising is a problem though especially if you forget one bit. You need an understanding to fill in the gaps. I try to understand by supplementing my notes but the pressure on the course does not allow for reflection...'

This student attempted taking a deep approach but found that a surface approach was what was rewarded:

Interviewer: 'What do you think the lecturers want?'
Student: 'It depends how much pressure you are under. If you are under a lot of pressure then you will just concentrate on passing the course. I know that from bitter experience. One subject I wasn't very good at I tried to understand the subject and I failed the exam. When I re-took the exam I just concentrated on passing the exam questions. I got 96 percent and the guy couldn't understand why I failed the first time. I told him this time I just concentrated on passing the exam rather than understanding the subject. I still don't understand the subject so it defeated the object in a way. In the ideal world you must learn but if you are under a lot of pressure then you've got to be a bit more mercenary about it.'

This student was asked what got the marks in coursework and what the lecturers wanted:

' ...more to do with factual information than anything else, to be fac-
tually right and short...seeing if you've got all the factual information
correct.'

Some students brought a surface approach with them when they arrived, but the
course did not challenge this approach but rather confirmed it:

'I memorise facts for examinations and I do need my notes to jog my
memory. I had a poor experience at BSc level and lacked motivation...simply
because I have been brought up since school to memorise facts just to get
through exams. I wish there was more time on the course (the Diploma)
for further enquiry.'

The lack of initiative in some students was also evident:

'... I depend very much on the lecturer and good notes are important
to me. I want to learn more and would like to have more references.
I need to be directed by the lecturer to where I can find the sources of
information.'

The problem was diagnosed as one of excessive curriculum content and passive
learning reinforced by an assessment system which rewarded regurgitation of material
not properly understood. One might expect the practical work, in this case field work
on board boats in the Tamar Estuary, to avoid these problems. However students
approached even practical work in an unreflective way, following instructions and
taking little initiative.

About 60 percent of the course studied here is practical work. In the past it had
been relatively unstructured. Students undertook measurements in the field under
staff supervision, essentially to generate some data, and subsequently attempted to
make sense of this data individually. Group co-operation was regarded with great
suspicion by the staff. Students were poorly motivated and considered practical work
as purely a way of gaining good marks rather than as a way of acquiring knowledge
and skills of value in obtaining a good job. The jaded abilities of the graduates
were recognised by industrial partners who were critical of students capabilities with
regard to:

- design and implementation of fieldwork;

- ability to link theory to results and to exploit data;

- report writing ability.

Students were frustrated by their lack of input into the design of fieldwork. Even
when they were asked to suggest methods, these were not used. Nevertheless the
potential of fieldwork for quality in learning was apparent to students:

'I think the fieldweeks are invaluable really, because I learn a lot more
in the fieldweeks than I do sitting in a lecture ...'

The innovation

Instead of working individually on a series of small teacher-set tasks, students were set up into teams and undertook three major projects in the form of 'real world' jobs.

1. Power station outfall

    This involved surveys of the Tamar Estuary to assess the potential damage of the discharge of thermal effluent into the Tamar by a power station planned by a power comapny, for which background data was available. The problem was posed in a letter from a 'client', together with the client's specifications. This project involved not only data gathering but also research into the ecological implications of the development. In addition students had to take a great deal of trouble to organise themselves for what was a complex multifaceted task.

2. Appraisal of oceanographic data

    A client had a requirement for data analysis which involved the design and validation of a user-friendly computer program which could be used in future deep-sea surveys where certain types of equipment are employed. Data was supplied by the client.

3. Appraisal of a topic of concern to a client

    Instead of a conventional essay, students were required to identify a topic in which the client's company may play a major role (eg the impact of the greenhouse effect on rising sea levels) research the topic and present a report to the client in a way the client could understand and use within the company.

Students were set up into groups of about ten and expected to assume responsibility for their surveys, the collection of supplementary information obtained from literature sources, and the interpretation of the results. The organisation of the survey in terms of student activities and the people they need to communicate with is described in Figure 10.1.

Each group carries out three surveys of the estuary once every three weeks during the Autumn term. When the group is not at sea it is expected to meet, during allocated times, to carry out data reduction or acquisition of the supplementary information. While it is a group task students are told that the project reports will be submitted individually. The groups meet with the 'client', (a role performed by the tutor) once every three weeks to discuss progress. The tutor also discusses reflective journals and skills reviews. This component of the innovation is designed to encourage group work and leadership skills and decision making about the deployment of human and physical resources. It is designed to give students insights into the way projects will be managed in industrial contexts. The surveys are backed with a substantial manual of background information, organisational details and a bibliography.

The lecture programme in parallel with the practical work has been rescheduled so that the theoretical treatment of environmental data now has a higher profile and comes early on so that it is placed firmly in the context of the practical work.

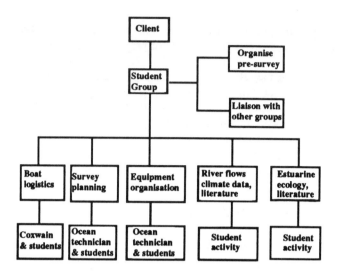

Figure 10.1: Organisation of student activities for fieldwork

Skill development

To develop computing skills the data generated in the field was integrated into student problem-solving. Students' awareness of data management and interpretation was developed through the more effective use of computers. Each student had his or her ability in computing (including word-processing, use of spreadsheets and use of graph packages) assessed at the start of the course by the lecturer. Then a weekly time allocation had to be spent on an individualised basis strengthening the areas of weakness. The students' progress was monitored and the quality of the first assignment (the appraisal of oceangraphic data, which was highly geared to computing) used to gauge the students' ability in computing.

A similar approach was taken in other assignment work where the students were asked to provide environmental impact statements on key data. In these cases, a link between research and teaching was essential in order that the latest practical approaches and theoretical concepts were incorporated into student thinking.

Written communication skills were developed via a series of structured tutorials and a manual, which was complemented by the development of a skills review for each individual. The skills review include the review of teamwork and interpersonal skills and was designed to help students to compile a *Curriculum Vitae* with a better awareness of the skills which they possessed.

A manual containing material to help students review their skills and develop their group work skills is being introduced.

Reflective journals

A reflective journal was also introduced, though with limited success. Students' 'fieldwork critiques' had tended to be a descriptive re-hash of the main fieldwork report and students had trouble with the concept of a reflective journal despite several discussion concerning the idea. Further steps are planned to provide students with the guidance and support necessary to make reflective journals work effectively (although extracts from journals, below, illustrate what is possible). Chapter 7 describes reflective journals being used very effectively by engineering students.

Assessment

Although they worked in teams, students submitted individual reports. Assessment criteria and the allocation of marks backed up the concern for skills. Marks were allocated in the following way:

1	Commitment to group activity and involvement in fieldwork:	15%
2	Development of computing:	15%
3	Background reading and research	15%
4	Quality of journal and skills review	25%
5	Quality of final report	30%

Table 10.1 summarises the differences between the course before and after the changes:

Before	After
Staff led survey work	Student led surveys
Poor group activities	Significant group activity
Academic exercises	Problem-based studies in real-work contexts
Weak application of theory and research ideas	Integration of theory with application and better involvement of library research
Data not fully exploited	Purposeful use of data via improved use of computers
Conventional laboratory report	Professional technical report
No skills review or reflection	Skills review and reflective journal

Table 10.1: 'Before' and 'After' changes to the course

In terms of the four key features which foster a deep approach this innovation contained the following elements:

Motivational context:

There was greater personal responsibility, both individual and collective, and involvement with industrially-relevant problems.

Interaction:

Students worked as a group, involving peer teaching and co-operation. In order to plan their practical work students were also involved in negotiations with academic and technical staff.

Learner activity:

Students undertook no more practical work but now they reflected on it to a greater extent, for example through the use of reflective journals. There was a greater emphasis on the development of skills, especially practical computing skills.

A well structured knowledge base:

There was greater involvement with current research topics in the marine environment leading to a clearer understanding of impact assessment. All the elements of a major study were integrated into one project rather than being divided up into separate technical components.

The study

The Approaches to Studying questionnaire was administered to students on the BSc Marine Studies version of the Oceanography course at the end of the year before the innovations were introduced, at the start of the innovation in the Autumn term, in the Spring term, and in the summer term shortly before exams. The results are shown in Table 10.2 below.

	Achieving	Reproducing	Meaning
Summer 1990 (Before: n = 17)	14.47	15.00	15.59
Autumn 1990 (Term 1: n = 36)	16.06	14.25	16.64
Spring 1991 (Term 2: n = 36)	16.53	12.75	17.19
Summer 1991 (Term 3: n = 36)	15.41	13.44	16.52

Table 10.2: Approaches to Studying scores of students on the Oceanography course the previous year, and at three points in the year

As can be seen, students motivation increased. It was already significantly higher in the Autumn term than the year before ($p < .01$) and increased further in the

Spring term. Students' surface approach was lower. By the Spring term it was significantly lower than the year before ($p < .001$) and lower than in the Autumn term ($p < .01$). Students' deep approach was significantly higher than the year before by the Spring term ($p < .001$). In other words all three indicators of the quality of student learning showed progressive improvements in the desired direction. However all three indicators also declined (though not significantly) in the summer term. By this time students had finished their practical work and were concentrating on revising for exams. The dominant demand on them was therefore very different to that during the field work and this is reflected in their reduced motivation, increased surface approach and reduced deep approach. This illustrates a phenomenon identified in several of the other case studies (cf Chapter 4) of students reverting to earlier patterns of learning as soon as they are confronted with conventional demands again.

These differences in students' approaches might have been due to the student cohort being different to that the year before or due to general improvements in the entire degree programme affecting all course components. To explore this possibility students on parallel courses in Marine Technology and Navigation were also surveyed. Table 10.3 compares students from these courses and also includes the scores from students on the course before the changes were introduced.

	Achieving	Reproducing	Meaning
Oceanography (Term 2: n = 36)	16.53	12.75	17.19
Oceanography (Before: n = 17)	14.47	15.00	15.59
Marine Technology (n = 19)	15.00	14.95	14.63
Navigation (n = 8)	15.50	15.75	12.75

Table 10.3: Approaches to Studying scores of students on the Oceanography course and two parallel courses

The ways students approached these two parallel courses were not significantly different from the Oceanography course before the innovations were introduced (with the exception of the Navigation course which had significantly lower deep-approach scores) but were both significantly worse on all three indicators in 1991. In other words while students continued to study on parallel courses as students had done in the previous year on the Oceanography course, they changed significantly on the Oceanography course once the innovations were introduced. The difference in deep approach scores between Oceanography and the two parallel courses is particularly marked.

The Approaches to Studying questionnaire was also administered to the Diploma students (Table 10.4).

	Achieving	Reproducing	Meaning
Summer 1990 (Before: n = 16)	15.56	16.62	14.94
Autumn 1990 (Term 1: n = 20)	15.50	15.30	16.55
Summer 1991 (Term 2: n = 20	15.85	16.35	17.15
Science norms	13.08	14.26	13.93

Table 10.4: Approaches to Studying scores of students on the Diploma course

The Diploma students' motivation was already at a high level and did not increase. Their surface approach scores were previously very high indeed (compared with norms for science students) and while they declined, this was not a significant decline and they increased again at the end of the year before exams, as the Degree students' approach scores had done. Their deep approach scores continued to increase to a high level significantly above that of the previous year ($p < .001$) and very considerably above the norm for science students.

The high level of the Diploma students' surface approach scores, significantly above that for the less mature Degree students, requires some explanation. The one-year Diploma course was perceived by the students to be too short and too full:

'Essentially we are trying to do something in one year that would take others two or three years. Unless you cram it with exams at the end its the only quick way to assess people in a short space of time'

They experienced a great deal of pressure, and passing the course and gaining the qualification was crucial to their careers. Despite their clear desire to understand, reflected in their high deep approach scores, the excessive size of the curriculum and the pressure of exams also induced a surface approach.

A sample of students was interviewed to explore their approaches in more depth. Their scores on the questionnaire were reflected in their interviews. For example:

Interviewer: 'What do you think the lecturers actually want when you are doing the coursework or problem solving?'
Student: 'The main priority is to sort of learn round the subject. I mean the major benefit of coursework is to actually go out yourself and learn about a particular subject in depth.'
Interviewer: 'But exactly what is it that the lecturers are after when they set you things to do?'
Student: 'Well I would guess that they are trying to see how you respond

to the task. How you can interpret the problem ... whether you are going to do the minimum that's necessary or whether you are going to develop the work more independently and have original ideas...'

Interviewer: 'Can I ask you when you are studying what you are actually doing?'

Student: 'I think I try to understand the basic principles, yes that's what I always do...I can't retain much of the information for a lot of the time ...but if I think I know...the basics...I can use that to develop ideas from there...I always end up sitting down with books and whatever trying to understand it.'

Interviewer: 'When you are in a lecture or you are problem solving what are you actually thinking about?'

Student: 'I think about how I am going to apply that to the job...I always look for applications...so its always building into my knowledge...I do follow up my interests as well besides the set work because when I'm reading something interesting I'll go and get more books on it and find out what it's about.'

Interviewer: 'When you do a piece of coursework what is it you think the lecturers are after?'

Student: 'Well, I think they are looking to see if you understand... You haven't just read a piece of work and regurgitated it on to paper...that you've really understood what you've read and you can apply it...they take into account that you understand and that you've answered the question...I try to get a fundamental understanding because I think this is important. A lot of articles are advanced but I still want to understand them.'

The way the practical work was linked to theoretical issues worked very effectively compared with the previously routine work, as illustrated in this reflective journal entry:

'...I found the field week 2 very useful to my knowledge of oceanography. My previous course was purely surveying, so this side of the industry was new to me. What was carried out prior to the week, during the week and then after the week put a lot of what was purely theoretical work into practical applications...'

The form the practical work took clearly affected students' independence and motivation:

'I should like to say that I was impressed by the way that this fieldweek was organised and run and I am glad to say that a lot was learned by myself. Perhaps most importantly of all if a similar survey had to be undertaken again I would feel a lot more confident second time around.'

'The logship exercise was the first part of the fieldweek of which I had absolutely no previous knowledge and as such was an interesting experience. Again a very simple procedure not a lot to go wrong. Accuracy tolerances are not high but adequate for the use to which the information would be put. I would be quite confident of carrying out a logship exercise on my own in the future.'

'I enjoyed organising the buoy fixing as it gave me something to plan, organise and conduct.'

Students expressed confidence in new abilities, such as data handling with computers:

'The drogue tracking and logship data gave me the opportunity to come to grips with Harvard Graphics, but as I became better with the package I became more valuable as a computer user.'

Students made many comments about the effects of the group work on their learning:

'In general the fieldwork went very well, mostly due to good back up and the fact that the group were left to organise themselves. It would appear that crew members are more willing to be punctual and diligent for their colleagues than they are for lecturers !'

'A small group of kindred spirits, with a task in hand and an enthusiasm for the job can produce excellent results in a harmonious atmosphere. Unfortunately, life only provides such situations on rare occasions as a tantalising glimpse of how things could be. My experience on this fieldweek, and particularly with the team was one of those glimpses. The world needs organisation and leaders.'

'...you learn a lot off group input when questions are being asked and the questions you ask as well. It's not just a one-way thing with a lecturer just teaching it to you. It's one thing I like about the group, there's a lot of group involvement, there's a lot of questions asked and you tend to learn a lot more from those questions than you would do from a lecturer.'

Not all group work is automatically successful. Experienced students sometimes commented that their group got more out of the projects than they did, and the following student commented on the organisation involved, in his reflective journal:

'I also found, yet again, the problems associated with group work, these being that (i) with too many people a lot gets said without the group getting anywhere and (ii) those individuals who don't get involved get carried along and receive the same amount of credit'.

Groups were as large as ten, which can cause management difficulties. Students submit individual reports as a way of combating the second point the student made, but careful attention to the way the assessment system supports or undermines group co-operation is vital. The external examiner also commented on the fairness of assessment of the outcomes of group work.

Students' experience on the Oceanography course had an affect on the way they responded to some of their parallel courses. For example the Diploma in Hydrographic Survey has several fieldweeks, the first of which is a survey of a local reservoir. A student wrote in his oceanography critical review:

> 'The principles of the oceanography field trip were easier to grasp and an adequate series of discussions preceded the operation. Thus, a much more egalitarian attitude prevailed where people did not have to feel inadequate because they did not have a clue about what was happening, which was the situation on Burrator (the reservoir survey).'

As a direct result of this and similar criticisms, the staff responsible for the reservoir survey have now revised it along the lines of the oceanography case study. The requirement for the mapping and bathymetry of the reservoir is to be presented to the students as a consultancy-based task for the local water company.

Learning outcomes

Evidence on the quality of learning outcomes was available from three sources: the assessment system, the external examiner, and employers.

The average marks of the BSc students on the course were very significantly higher: 67% compared with 55% the previous year ($p < .001$). Analysis of Diploma students' individual project reports using the SOLO taxonomy also showed a dramatic change in the quality of their work. Table 12.2 shows that only 27% of reports (4 out of 15) the previous year were at SOLO levels 3 and above, whereas after the introduction of the changes 90% of the reports (18 out of 20) were at this level. Previously no reports were at the highest SOLO level whereas three were at level 5 after the changes. One of the reports was taken on a national tour in the form of an exhibition. The difference in the pattern of results in this table is highly significant ($\mathcal{X}^2 = 15.08$, $d.f. = 2$, $p < .001$).

The postgraduate Diploma students also produced two group reports: one at SOLO level 4 and one at SOLO level 5. They were considered the best the course had ever produced and the latter contained an innovative scheme for the management of the power station in respect of the environmental protection of the Tamar Estuary. This led directly to the employment of one of the group's members in the Tidal Waters Division of the local National Rivers Authority.

The external examiner commented:

> 'The overall standard of the students on this one year course is high. A very uniformly high standard was achieved in the practical work. This

SOLO level	1990	1991
1	4	0
2	7	2
3	3	10
4	1	5
5	0	3

Table 10.5: Number of students' reports at each level of the SOLO taxonomy

is in part due to the fact that much of the work is done in groups. The quality of the course as a whole is very high. A re-validation of the course by the RICS earlier this year commented on the high standards and relevance of the course.'

In an interview, an employer of two students who had been through the course, one three years before (here labelled *A*), and one who had experienced the revised course (*B*), described the difference between them:

Interviewer: 'I am interested in your opinions of *A* and *B*. Could you compare them?'
Employer: '*B* is definitely the best of the two by a long way. *A* is next to useless despite the fact that he has been here for three years. *A* lacks initiative, he is slow and is not intellectually up to the job. There is little good to say.'
Interviewer: 'What are the special attributes which you regard as important in *B*?'
Employer: '*B*'s capabilities have been developed to a high state. He is very capable in the field. He has the ability to get to the nitty gritty in all our operations. He has shown a very mature approach and he takes the initiative. We have been so confident with him that he is putting together contracts. He has gone straight in and he was producing good work within a fortnight.'

In order to gain an even fuller picture of the changes in learning outcomes brought about by the course other staff involved will also be interviewed as to their perceptions on whether they felt the quality of learning had improved. Finally, it is intended to provide a long-term follow through of selected students in terms of the attitudes of employers.

Conclusions

Through a series of interrelated innovations the quality of students' approaches to learning, and their learning outcomes, were markedly improved on one course taught as part of two programmes. The key features of these innovations were:

112

- problem-based learning;

- interaction in co-operative groups;

- well structured development of the necessary technical, interpersonal and communication skills;

- assessment criteria congruent with the above features.

Problems within the course which remain to be tackled include improving students' ability to use the reflective journal effectively and the further development of a manual and mechanisms to support and monitor students' group and organisational skills.

The major problems, however, lie outside the course in the overall Degree and Diploma programmes. The conventional demands of these courses, and especially the conventional assessment demands, limit the impact and duration of the improvements in students' learning. Until the changes become more widely adopted, the improvements may remain localised. While attempts to sell the innovation have been made through several sessions with other staff and a presentation made to the Faculty Board on approaches to studying and monitoring quality, no widespread change has yet occurred. For the time being students will be confronted with incompatible demands, especially from the assessment, on different course elements.

There have been objections from staff to the use of independent group learning and peer tutoring, on the grounds that it might pave the way for a reduction in staffing. Students also fear that they might not get good value for money:

'Experienced students pay through the nose to be taught, not to be teachers...'

Until decisions about how courses should be taught and are made on the grounds of quality in learning there may be little scope for further progress.

Chapter 11

Interdisciplinary studies in Physiotherapy

Innovator: Kay Stachura, The Queen's College, Glasgow

This case study describes a range of innovations in an 'Integrated Professional Studies' programme in the final year of a BSc Physiotherapy course. While it was possible to identify extensive qualitative changes in student learning, there was no change as measured by the Approached to Studying questionnaire. The possible reasons for this are explored.

Context

The BSc Physiotherapy Course at The Queen's College, Glasgow, is a three year degree course with an annual student intake of 90 students. Integrated Professional Studies (IPS) is taught in each year of the course and aims to encourage students to synthesise theoretical knowledge and professional skills acquired in the other subject areas in the course in order that they may develop a holistic approach towards the treatments and management of patients. It is IPS in the third year of the course which is the basis of the current research project.

Prior to the introduction of the new IPS programme, all teaching in this subject in the third year of the course was conducted by means of a twelve week lecture programme given predominately by external lecturers. Each weekly programme involved three hours teaching. Each programme covered various aspects of the treatment and management of specific patient groups, for example, the elderly and the young chronic sick. There was much duplication of content and very little variety in teaching methods. This repetitive format appeared to encourage a surface approach to learning. The lecturers each tended to focus on a specific pathology. This encouraged a prescriptive approach to patient care with little inter-relating of ideas between the various patient groups concerned. This prescriptive approach and emphasis on

	Achieving	Reproducing	Meaning
IPS, end of year 2 (n = 70)	13.00	14.70	13.90
Social Science norms	12.73	13.65	14.21

Table 11.1: Mean scores for IPS year 2 students on the Approaches to Studying questionnaire

factual detail encouraged students to adopt a pathology-based approach to patient care and focus on the symptom presentation, attempting to memorise the appropriate techniques which should be employed to treat particular symptoms.

Assessment consisted of one piece of course work which took the form of a 5,000 word independent study assignment and two 3-hour traditional examinations at the end of the academic year. There was no revision time included as part of the programme. The only form of support teaching offered was as part of the students' clinical experience when topics might be discussed in relation to placements. There was no estimation of the number of independent study hours required to achieve the objectives of the IPS programme and no timetabled private study time allocated to the students.

The absence of an underlying conceptual framework to the Third Year IPS programme meant that the subject was not fulfilling its integrative function as well as it might. This was particularly true for the Behavioural Science component. In many aspects, the lecture programme format in the third year of the course was similar to the IPS programme taught in the second year. However, the third year IPS programme was not supported by tutorials where ideas could be explored in greater depth.

Prior to the commencement of the new IPS programme the Approaches to Studying questionnaire was administered to second year students and a sample of students, selected to represent a range of levels of coursework performance, were interviewed. The students displayed a significantly higher Reproducing score than national norms for social science students ($p < .01$). The Achieving and Meaning scores were not significantly different (Table 11.1).

The following student described the compartmentalised approach to the material which the IPS course was meant to avoid:

Interviewer:'Yes, but what does learning mean?'
Student: 'I think I've got to sit down and go over it. I've got to go over it quite a lot before I can actually get into it... to remember it. After my initial stage I'll take notes then read over them. Get them in my mind. Break it up, bit by bit as I go along.'
Interviewer: 'When you're at the "bit by bit" stage what are you doing?'
Student: '... take all the information you've highlighted about that sec-

tion, I think I've to memorise things to sort of remember things... to memorise. That's the way I sort of learn.'

The following student illustrated a clear surface approach to another subject:

Student: 'In Anatomy, it's the basic knowledge that's required. I'd read it and them try and summarise what I've read. Put it into my own words and reproduce it.'
Interviewer: 'So, you aim to reproduce...?'
Student: 'You see, I don't like reading. I find it really tedious because... I don't know why I don't like it... The way I know I've learnt what I've read is by being able to write down what I've read... reading it, thinking about it and writing it down again. That way I know I've learnt it.'
Interviewer: 'So, with this material that you've written down... What do you aim to do with it?'
Student: 'Reproduce it. Put it down again.'

If students were to integrate different subjects and take an interdisciplinary approach to the treatment and management of patients then a surface approach had to be avoided.

Innovation

Two main changes were introduced to the IPS programme to improve the quality of student learning:

1. A thematic approach was adopted in order to provide a more cohesive conceptual framework for the separate components of the course. A 'care' ethic was highlighted, in contrast to a 'cure' ethic. When dealing with the treatment of clinical pathologies students were introduced to different approaches, for example contrasting a biopsychosocial approach to a purely therapeutic approach. Students were encouraged to critically evaluate clinical management practices from these different perspectives rather than to memorise appropriate techniques.

2. A variety of different teaching strategies was introduced with the intention of more actively involving the students in their own learning. It was considered important that the teaching methods should engage the students' affect and well as their intellect, and so reflect the widening focus of the content of the course. To engage students' feelings and to change their attitudes required more active learning and more reflection than had previously been common. Students needed to reflect on the significance and application of the new concepts to their clinical experience and practice.

The particular needs of specific patient groups who suffered from chronic pathologies still had to be covered by the course to allow students to complete their clinical placements.

The aims and objectives of the new IPS programme are listed in full below in order to illustrate the extent to which higher-order conceptual aims were dominant over lower-order procedural aims.

Aims

1. To encourage the implementation of a broader perspective in clinical practice.

2. To enable students to identify the characteristic features of different models of patient care.

3. To enable students to critically evaluate current management practices at both individual treatment level and at a more general management level.

Objectives

1. Synthesise knowledge of applied anatomy, physiology, behavioural science, pharmacology, medical and surgical procedures.

2. Extract, interpret and clinically evaluate patient data and demonstrate an ability to integrate this knowledge into the provision of a realistic programme

3. Identify and critically appraise the parameters and assessment procedures used to evaluate particular problems with which the physiotherapist must be familiar in order to provide effective intervention.

4. Discuss the selection, application and modification of physiotherapy procedures for different patient groups.

5. Demonstrate an understanding of the various roles undertaken by the physiotherapist as part of his/her clinical practice.

6. Develop an understanding and an ability to identify the different characteristics of a 'care' and 'cure' ethic in programmes of patient management.

7. Discuss the importance of the environment in rehabilitation and identify factors which contribute towards the creation of a therapeutic environment.

8. Demonstrate a knowledge of the various factors which can compromise the patient's ability to respond fully to physiotherapy intervention; identify particular patient groups where this might be a problem and suggest strategies to help overcome such problems.

9. Develop a basic understanding of the stages in the acquisition or refinement of motor skills and demonstrate an awareness of the various stages in their instruction and presentation to the patient.

117

In order to achieve the above aims a variety of teaching methods were employed:

1. Keynote Lectures

   Lectures from experienced practitioners were retained where they could be used to synthesise information: for example lectures by physiotherapists giving an overview of practice with a particular client group. Occasionally these lectures took the form of informal talks on controversial issues such as sexuality and the physically disabled person and personal accounts of what it is like to be physically disabled. The lectures were intended to be interactive.

2. Resource Packages

   A set of six resource packages was produced, one for each module on the IPS programme. Each contained a series of articles and a set of questions designed to encourage reflection on the articles. 20 hours of private study time was timetabled for students to work on these packages. The articles were selected primarily to illustrate the way a range of disciplines dealt with the concepts encountered on the programme and it was intended that they would help students to make the necessary links between the IPS programme and their clinical practice while on placement

3. Visit

   The programme included a half-day visit to an Adult Training Centres to give students first hand experience of the management of adults with special educational needs. Both the environment and the client group were quite new to the students. Students' personal reactions to working with these clients and their understanding of the philosophy and methods used at the Centre were debriefed in a session following the visit.

4. Workshops

   Workshops were included on two occasions in the programme to encourage greater student involvement and motivation. Use was made of appropriate video material in these workshops allowing the inclusion of real-world situations and students were set a variety of problem-based exercises making use of the video materials and drawing on the student's existing knowledge and experience.

   The workshop in Term 1 included a debriefing session on the students' visit. The debriefing session was conducted initially by the students on their own and subsequently with the tutor. The programme for this workshop is reproduced below.

IPS Workshop	
9.15	Session 1 Awareness raising video on aspects of mental handicap.
10.00	Coffee
10.15	Session 2 Reflection session This session will involve students reflecting on their responses to the video and the experience of their visit to the Adult Training Centres. The session will be loosely structured and possible areas to consider will be suggested. This will provide a loose structure for the third session.
11.15	Session 3 Students will gather in their work groups with their tutor who will collate the experiences of the groups, under the headings suggested in session 2.
11.50	Session 4 Working in mental handicap A physiotherapist working in the field of mental handicap will share her perceptions of her work with the group.
12.15	End

5. Group Tasks

Students were allocated to work groups. Each work group was allocated a simulation task to undertake which drew on students' knowledge and skills acquired earlier in the programme. The simulation tasks involved students taking the role of the carer of a client, or the role of a physiotherapist, and engaging in setting up a 'carer's meeting' and the simulated tackling of the problems encountered while caring for a particular client group. Students were familiar with the pathologies associated with client groups but are not used to taking the perspective of the client or of carers. Students had to co-operate in delegating and sharing tasks and in preparing a presentation. 12 hours were allocated to this group task and three hours to a session in which groups presented the outcomes of their work.

6. Seminars

Student work groups were each allocated a tutor for seminar sessions. These varied in format and included debriefings on clinical experience and open discussion of issues raised by students while on clinical placements. On occasion the groups worked in sub-groups for discussion. Although 14 hours was allocated to these discussions, only two thirds of these hours were actually used for seminars. The final seminar session was spent reviewing previous IPS exam questions and a debriefing session was carried out at the end of the seminar programme.

Assessment

Assessment on the third year of the IPS had consisted of one 5,000 word assignment and two three-hour examinations. This format was retained but the exam questions were changed in format. Instead of conventional questions a 'modified essay question' format was adopted. This involved a description of a situation followed by a series of detailed questions which take students through steps of analysis and decision making about a complex problem. This was intended to encourage a more problem-solving approach.

Key features

The key features of the IPS programme intended to foster a deep approach were:

- a well-structured knowledge base. The theme-based approach was designed to build on students' existing clinical knowledge and experience to provide a coherent conceptual framework.

- active learning, including role play and a visit;

- interaction, in workshops, group tasks and seminars.

The main teaching and learning strategies adopted were:

- learning by doing, through the group tasks, visit and workshops;

- problem-based learning, in that the starting point for learning was usually clinical situations;

- personal development, in that students were encouraged to explore their personal reactions to clients and their attitudes to contentious issues, not just knowledge and skills;

- reflection on students' clinical experience, the videos and the experiential activities.

The whole course was designed to break students out of what had traditionally been a prescriptive approach and to encourage a more sensitive and empathetic approach to clients based on an interdisciplinary understanding.

The total amount of students' time spent in class declined from 20 hours a week in year one to 12 hours a week in year three. Of this 12 hours, six were allocated to the IPS programme in an intensive one-day slot each week when students were not on clinical placements.

Introducing the innovation

One lecturer produced the first of the resource packages as a model and then a team of four co-operated to produce the others. It took a good deal of time and involved a range of practical problems, including copyright clearance, reprographics, and the co-operation of the inter-library loan staff and Educational Development Unit. Additional lecturers were initially brought into the team to run the programme, as a staff development exercise. Co-operation within a team was considered a considerable bonus of the innovation.

The study

The Approaches to Studying questionnaire was administered at the end of the first and second terms. Students were selected to be interviewed on the basis of their scores on the questionnaire: students with distinct approaches were identified in order to explore a range of reactions to the course. In addition an independent evaluation was undertaken by the Educational Development Unit. This evaluation found that students perceived the IPS programme quite differently from their previous experience on the course. For example:

'IPS is totally different to the second year. It's not just pathologies. It's about thinking rather than memorising.'

In the interviews students found the IPS programme having an impact on their thinking during their clinical practice.

'I'm now starting to make my own decisions of what social history I ask and why I ask it, because sometimes I don't see the relevance of the social history. Up to the beginning of the third year I'd have been asking it because you should be asking it. Now, I ask it because I know what I'm looking for.'

Another student, when asked to describe the effect of the IPS programme on her practice, commented:

Student: 'It's increased my understanding when I've been dealing with somebody... but not necessarily my knowledge.'
Interviewer: 'Do you see a difference between learning and knowledge?'
Student: 'Yes. All I can do is relate it back to clinical practice. I knew about things in second year but I didn't know how to use it.'

It was common for students to contrast the form of learning on the IPS programme to that in previous years:

Student: '... text book stuff... you read it and you think, well that's that! I mean, when you're reading it, it's more difficult to branch out into real-life... I wonder whether it's just a processing thing you do rather than a learning thing from the information.'
Interviewer: 'You're saying: "it's a processing thing rather than a learning thing?" Do you feel you've done more "processing" this year or more "learning"?'
Student: '... probably more learning, I would say. I think that's the

positive sign. That if you've actually used it there has been some learning experience going on... I feel a lot of the stuff this year is sort of clear... I seem to be using it more. That's how I judge learning, in that I seem to be using it and I'm aware of it.'

'In third year in some way you're just trying to widen your outlook rather than just focussing on your knowledge. You have to expand. I think in second year you're actually there just being taught. Probably it's the fact that you're not thinking about it. I know myself, in second year I wouldn't have looked into it in greater detail.'

Student: '(in the second year) I think I was aiming first to get hard facts, the pathology, the treatment. All the sort of stuff that you would actually use on clinical 'cause that was maybe the first time you would actually be going out and you could put it towards that.'
Interviewer: 'What were you aiming to do with the information?'
Student: 'You're trying to learn it.'
Interviewer: 'What do you mean by learn?'
Student: 'Memorise it. So that I can recall it if I need it.'
Interviewer: 'So, do you feel a difference in what you're trying to do now?'
Student: 'Integrate it together. Take another view other than the hard facts that you have to learn for sort of clinical placements. Things that you can actually think deeper about yourself...'
Interviewer: 'So, you find you're more involved in the process? Is that a change from Second year?'
Student: 'Yes, definitely. Because it was very much a factual thing, remembering different obstetric terms etc. Whereas it's easier to remember things this year... You're remembering them because they're so relevant that you do remember them. Rather than sitting there thinking, I've to remember, blah, blah, blah.'

A number of students commented that they were building on their previous knowledge:

'It's a cyclic thing. You've got knowledge which is your base and then you take knowledge from that base to learn, and as you learn you accumulate more knowledge. I wouldn't say I've gained a great volume of information. It's a sort of 're-use' of information in a different way. You know, using the knowledge you have in a different way. There has been, like bits and pieces that are totally new, but I think it's more using of the knowledge things that you've used in the past. But you're re-thinking it this year ... '

'It's more focussing towards clinical... how you would respond in different ways. Not just how you would go about treating someone. I see a difference in the focus from previous years' course. It's building on top of the basics we've already had.'

In conjunction with this idea of building on previous knowledge, students also talked about a widening of their ideas and increased awareness.

'I didn't see it at all as amassing information. It was bringing together things I already knew... taking a look at what you already know and maybe learning a bit more. It allows you to step back and look at it differently. It's more the quality of what I know that's increased rather than the quantity.'

Student: 'I'm less book-oriented. I'm more person-oriented. It seems to have widened... I'm trying to take a whole view rather than a single thing.'
Interviewer: 'Is it wider in the sense that you're amassing more information?'
Student: 'No. No. ...I think it's more an increased awareness. I think now I can explore more things.'

Students were not always happy about the changes. The following student was worried that her increased ability wasn't necessarily going to help her in the exams. The impact of the assessment system is an issue which will be raised again below.

'This actually bothers me when I look back... when we're talking about revising I can't actually identify things, facts, that I've learnt in third year apart from I feel as a person I'm far more able to go to speak to an elderly patient... to deal with a child, the carers or the family.'

The students interviewed certainly appeared to be aware of the impact of the IPS programme. They commented particularly on it's relevance to their clinical practice. Students were able to carry their learning from college into clinical practice and also bring their clinical experiences back into college. There was evidence from the interviews of students relating concepts and information acquired from lectures or from articles to patients' problems. For example:

'I try and relate it (information) to my placements and patients rather than just remembering it. I find it easier to think of a patient.'

'To begin with I was taking down too much (information). I take down main points, headings, words that I wasn't sure of, details of a patient I had thought of in that situation... that would remind me of it.'

The following student recognised the difference between IPS in the third year and her earlier studying, but seems to have preferred it when everything was done for her:

'Well, I quite like some self-learning but it's more sort of self-discipline as well. To try and actually go to the library and try and use the work-books. Whereas in the first and second years you were actually maybe getting more taught, more spoon-fed than what you're getting in third year. In a way, maybe that's a bit easier because if you've got classes you know you go to them and then get the information. Whereas, in the workbooks you've got to use it yourself, in your own time and you've to work out the time. Whereas, in the classes it's more sort of hard facts rather than using articles.'

The independent assessment carried out at the end of the academic year, reported:

'The workbooks were not seen as a success but neither were they branded as a failure. The general belief was that further development was necessary.'

Students used to memorising information were initially confused about what they were supposed to be doing with so much information in the workbooks. Several students described the process of discovering the purpose of learning.

Student: 'Before I started I felt there's no way I can learn this. I felt I was supposed to learn it. I felt I was supposed to gain statistics of how many elderly people fall, how they fall, why they fall...'
Interviewer: 'So did you think you'd to memorise from the packages at the beginning?'
Student: 'Yes. Yes I did... I thought... Well, I don't see what I'm going to gain. I don't understand why I'm doing this and I don't even feel I could remember it if I did. I just felt it was a waste of time initially. Then, I realised what you were after and what the point was.'
Interviewer: 'What was the point? Tell me.'
Student: 'Which was, well really to get a better understanding of the patient and be more aware of the circumstances surrounding perhaps the elderly, the mentally handicapped ... The questions at the end, there-fore, were really helpful but I feel maybe they should have come at the beginning of the article to encourage you to 'bear in mind the following factors' or something like that.'

So, far from encouraging the students to adopt a wider perspective and perhaps a qualitatively better approach to their practice, the resource package could have been encouraging some students to memorise. The need for more guidance in the use of the resource packages was a marked feature of the interviews.

The questions at the back of the packages worked well for some, though they felt under time pressure.

'I find they made you think 'cause at the end of each article or group of articles you had the questions saying look up this, look up that or think

124

about this... there was a learning experience going on. I think it is just the way you use it and if you had the time to use them properly. I can see the idea behind them. It's just the time factor involved with it, that seemed to cancel it out.'

That the IPS programme was relevant and interesting were seen to be key factors in stimulating students to learn. It had also been an intention of the programme to engage the students' affect as well as their intellect. Students responded favourably to this strategy, commenting that it not only made things easier to remember but that it also increased their insight into situations and allowed them to grow as people. One student discussed the effect of the Adult Training Centre visit.

'I'd otherwise have had a superficial approach to it (mental handicap), "Yes, I know what it's like" sort of thing. I wouldn't have known unless I'd experienced it like that. I was learning more about people. I wasn't shocked at the people, but at my own reactions.'

Another student discussed the effect a personal account of disability had on her.

'You could hear a personal account of what they actually went through... talking to you, telling you how they felt. Sort of feelings rather than someone who wasn't handicapped. You could relate better to the problem. That was interesting... You got involved. You weren't just sitting there listening.'

Students were asked if the student-led seminars when they shared their experiences, provided them with a useful learning experience.

'I found these times helpful. We'd talk about it. It's like having a superficial opinion and thinking you know about it. ... '

Another student described the structure in the third year as the best of the three.

Student: 'It's a maturation process and you're allowed that freedom. Freedom to mature within the third year.'
Interviewer: 'Tell me.'
Student: 'Well, for example, giving the discussions back to you (the students). Sitting discussing in groups without a lecturer guiding you sort of thing. We can go off and come back later and perhaps seeing what we've come up with.'
Interviewer: 'That sort of thing helps?'
Student: 'I think it does. I think other people's ideas, following up things that maybe you haven't thought of before. It makes you think.'
Interviewer: 'Why is it different if a lecturer sits there or not?'
Student: 'I think it comes down to whether it's within yourself or not. I mean, if you're just hearing them. Although you think you might be listening. Whereas if you're actually doing your own thought processes it tends to stick.'

The theme of personal growth is taken up again by the following students.

Interviewer: 'So, you're telling me that there's been a definite change in you?'

Student: 'Yes. Like a growing in me, a maturing in me. I've learned more about myself. Learned how to cope in different situations and getting confidence to go and alter my approach to people.'

(Student's Reproducing scale score=10, Meaning score=18)

Interviewer: 'Do you feel this year's IPS structure affects the way you go about your work?'

Student: 'I feel I've learnt... I've done much more work. I feel I've had to do more work. Perhaps it's because I've got independent study time. I feel I'm learning more... I'm definitely developing much more. I'm starting to find that rather than just having a collection of facts about a certain pathology or something like that I'm bringing everything together. You've got to think about everything. I'm definitely having to think much more than I did in the past.'

Interviewer: 'Do you feel any qualitative changes this year?'

Student: 'I feel I'm learning more myself.'

Interviewer: 'In what ways?'

Student: 'Before you would tend to get work and you would just do it. Now I'm more involved in what I'm doing. I'm enjoying it much better.'

In general the IPS programme seemed to involve students at a personal level in a way which was new for them. Students used words like 'powerful' to discuss certain IPS sessions, for example, the workshop on carers. As an example of their strong personal responses, some students asked for a debriefing session after a short presentation from two physically handicapped young men. They felt that the comments the young men had made about attitudes towards disability were appropriate for society in general, but were inappropriate to apply to them. Much heated debate went on and students were encouraged to reflect on why they thought the young men had taken such a contentious standpoint. There was qualitative evidence that students were being more reflective in relation to clinical practice. This had been commented on by both clinical and college staff. For example students attempted to involve carers more in the rehabilitation programmes even though some of practising clinicians, perhaps, favoured a more traditional, prescriptive approach to patient care.

The above interview data gives an impression of an extensive impact on students and on the quality of their learning. They were able to recognise the difference between the demands the course previously made and to describe improvements in their learning. However, this encouraging qualitative picture was not mirrored in students' responses to the Approaches to Studying questionnaire.

	Achieving	Reproducing	Meaning
IPS, year 3, term 1 (n = 70)	13.7	14.8	13.8
IPS, year 3, term 2 (n = 70)	13.8	14.3	14.3
IPS, end of year 2 (n = 70)	13.0	14.7	13.9

Table 11.2: Mean scores for IPS year 3 students on the Approaches To Studying Questionnaire

Analysis of the questionnaire data

As the Table 11.2 shows, students did not change their approach over the course of the first two terms. Furthermore their approach in the final year did not differ from their approach in the second year.

There was an apparent discrepancy between the qualitative data and observations of those involved, on the one hand, and the data from the Approaches to Studying questionnaire on the other. Many of the students' interview statements which revealed a deep approach concerned their clinical practice and their personal development. There are no items on the questionnaire which would pick this up. On the other hand where they talked about academic studying—lectures, note-taking, reading and preparing for the exam, which the questionnaire taps—their deep approach was much less clear-cut and many students revealed an ambivalent attitude. It seems likely that the students' approach was affected primarily in relation to understanding their clinical experience rather than in relation to formal study tasks. It is important to understand why students failed to adopt a deeper approach to studying and why they did not abandon a surface approach.

The new programme was introduced into the final year of a very information-heavy, three-year unclassified degree programme. Students' timetables were very full—they even had clinical placements over the summer holiday period. The unclassified degree course involved 115 weeks of study: only about 15 weeks short of a four year course. The overall workload may have been excessive. In addition students' study patterns may well have been too firmly established and they were unlikely to change a pattern which had succeeded in getting them through the first two years.

The stronger students had successfully adapted to the changing demands of the course. For example, the following student identified a difference in her approach from the first year:

'I try pinpoint in my mind a particular salient point. When I look back at first year, I tried to take everything in and now I realise that that's not necessary. I'm more relaxed and I know that I can take a more general

127

overview' (Student's Meaning scale score = 19, Reproducing scale score = 15)

As identified in interview extracts earlier, however, many students found the lack of hard facts on the IPS disorienting and failed to adjust their approach to learning appropriately.

The workbooks also caused problems. Students unused to independent learning were unsure what to do with the large amounts of material they contained and its sheer volume added to the work pressure, as illustrated by this student:

> 'I think the problem at the beginning was that I was trying to get through the reading. All I was doing, like the rest of us, was trying to get through the workbooks. Then I just stopped because there's no way ... I know we were told they're for over three terms, but I think ... I mean everybody was the same trying to get through them. There was this pressure.'
> (Students' Reproducing score = 16).

Even when students normally took a deep approach they seemed to lack the experience of tackling unstructured learning tasks to cope with the workbooks:

> Student: 'I feel it's too unstructured. When I saw the first IPS module and I saw the thickness of it ... then I saw the rest that needed doing... I didn't know where to start, where to begin, what they were looking for. Perhaps it's a bit stupid... I didn't realise that the questions at the back were really guidance questions. I thought they were like an assessment of what you'd remembered.'
> (Student's Reproducing score = 10, Meaning score = 18)

Some students simply took a surface approach to the task of reading the workbooks:

> Interviewer: 'What sort of things were you thinking about with the various bits of information you got from any particular article?'
> Student: 'To try and remember it. To try and use it. Just to write it down, 'cause very often when I'm reading I find that I'm not taking it in. So, I find by writing it down it helps me to take it in. It helps me to remember it.'

There were also practical problems with the production of the resource packages. To meet copyright requirements and to keep reprographics costs down the packages were deposited in the library. Students did not have their own copy to work with, to write notes on, and so on, and this may have encouraged students to treat them more reverentially, like books, rather than as working documents. That 50 percent of the packages disappeared from the library indicates the value to students of having their own copy.

Simply providing students with learning resources to replace or supplement lectures does not, on its own, induce a deep approach, whatever the content of the resources. Excessive amounts of material can just as easily induce a surface approach. If such workbooks are to be effective they need to be accompanied by learning activities, possibly backed up by discussion in class time, which encourage students to process the material actively. The less experienced are the students in tackling independent reading, the more structured help they will need. Students also need the study time, which is necessary for this active processing to take place, to be made available.

The assessment system did not change to support the other changes on the course, apart from the use of modified exam questions. This style of exam question is perhaps better suited to medical education where students are asked to analyse and synthesise information in patients' case histories in order to reach a diagnosis. However, Physiotherapy students are given the diagnosis. The intention behind the use of this question format was to try and encourage students' problem-solving skills. However the fragmented nature of the questions led to fragmented answers. There was a tendency to deal with each section of a question and not to inter-relate the various sections into a cohesive whole. They did not encourage students to try and develop their own arguments by drawing on the information and concepts covered in the IPS programme. Students tended to include key-words, like 'Biopsychosocial', without any development of what the term implies in the context of the question. In terms of the SOLO taxonomy the majority of answers were multistructural, listing the various rehabilitation options in each section. The better students tried to inter-relate some of their ideas, but there was little beyond this. The question format may have encouraged multistructural answers.

Lectures were retained. They were held in a banked lecture theatre and the skills of visiting speakers did not often include the ability to foster interaction with a large audience in such a room. While the visiting speakers were briefed, they did not explicitly reinforce the conceptual approach the IPS course was trying to develop. On two occasions three lectures were held in the space of a morning. It seems likely that such lecturing did not encourage active learning and did not present a coherent conceptual framework.

In order to foster a deeper approach the following changes are likely to be necessary:

- reducing the number and changing the nature of lectures so that their content and process more closely matches the philosophy of the course;

- changing the nature of the assessment so that it reinforces an analytic approach to physiotherapy problems;

- reducing the overall workload so that students have time to deal with material in depth;

- casting the material in the workbooks within a framework of tasks, questions and discussion in a way which fosters active learning;

- introducing active learning and more analysis and reflection at an earlier stage in the course so that students do not arrive in the third year with well established surface approaches.

Assessment

There was no improvement in students' coursework or exam marks and no improvement in clinical assessment marks. As described above, the majority of students' exam answers were 'multistructural' in SOLO terms and did not reveal the kind of awareness and analysis which students displayed in their interviews.

Developments

The IPS programme and its philosophy and methods acted as a springboard for the development of a four year Honours degree programme which received formal validation in 1991. The adoption of a thematic approach in the choice of subject material to highlight the integrative nature of IPS, and the emphasis on problem solving and the use of a range of student-centred teaching methods, have been replicated in the design of the final two years of the new course. There will only be one subject taught in the final two years: Issues in Physiotherapy Practice. A variety of themes will be considered within this subject, for example: Aspects of Health Promotion; Considerations in Management; Exploring Physiotherapeutics.

The other important outcome for the Honours course development was the changes made in clinical assessment. Inclusion of Clinical Studies within the classification for Honours necessitated changes in both the process of clinical education and assessment. There was a need to demonstrate that the clinical assessment displayed the same academic rigour demanded of the other components of assessment contributing to the Honours classification. Eleven placements will be assessed. The clinicians will assess students with a tutor and then an academic tutor will conduct a semi-structured interview with the student. The assessment of the content and quality of the students' responses determine if a higher grade should be awarded than that achieved by the clinicians' assessment. The SOLO taxonomy has provided a valuable framework for structuring the analysis of students' responses.

The School of Physiotherapy has embarked on a staff development exercise to familiarise staff with the SOLO taxonomy and how it provide a useful tool to help analyse students' responses. The advantages of this new assessment structure are that it should allow greater consistency in assessing students as all staff will be using the same framework. It will examine students' theoretical knowledge more rigorously than in the unclassified degree assessment and will go beyond the assessment of practical competency level which tended to dominate the unclassified degree programme.

In an attempt to address the potential problem of students being compromised clinically for attempting to implement innovative ideas developed on the IPS programme, the course team is organising a programme of continuing education for clinicians where ideas can be exchanged and the course philosophy reinforced. A discussion of the rationale and content of the IPS programme will be included in this programme.

The study undertaken to review the IPS programme described here will be repeated to evaluate the impact of the new Honours programme and, in particular, to see if changes have the desired effect on students' approaches to learning.

Conclusions

The IPS programme cut down on class contact, increased interaction, including interaction in tutor-less groups, increased active and experiential learning and provided a conceptual framework within which students were encouraged to address clinical situations and problems. Students were encouraged to undertake independent reading of specially prepared resource packs and to reflect on their personal reactions to client groups and to their clinical experience.

These innovations had a marked effect on students, many of whom recognised the difference between their earlier studies and how they were learning, and being encouraged to learn, on the third year IPS programme. Some of the impact of the programme was at a very personal level, with students recognising their own growing maturity. Academic and clinical staff have recognised the difference in students.

However, the accumulated effect of the teaching and assessment in the first two years had left students with a surface approach to academic study tasks which they carried over to their reading and to the way they tackled the examination questions. These study habits dominated students' approach to academic tasks and the Approaches to Studying questionnaire showed no overall changes in their approach.

What has been learnt from implementing the IPS programme has been used to develop a four-year Honours course, which has been successfully validated, and to introduce changes to the assessment of clinical practice which will involve a measure of the quality of students' understanding. However, if the first two years of the course remain unchanged, the surface approach which they induce may threaten the impact of the new developments in years three and four.

Chapter 12

Independent group project work in first year Business Law

Innovator: Brian Mitchell, Wolverhampton Polytechnic

This case study examines a first year Business Law module in which students undertook a series of six projects in independent groups. The projects involved a range of 'real world' tasks. Class contact time was used to support the groups and brief students for the projects rather than to present legal information. The innovation had a beneficial effect on students' approaches to studying and motivation once it had been 'fine-tuned'.

Context

The module studied here was a one-semester module forming part of the first year of a BA/BSc Business Information Systems course, and also taken by students from other subject areas. The module ran twice a year, involving students for about a quarter of their time for half a year. The aims of the module were:

'To develop knowledge and understanding of:

1. the legal institutions through which business disputes are resolved;

2. the legal environment in which businesses are established and in which they conduct their business; and

3. to develop skills of research, time management, communication, group work, information technology and the use of personal initiative.'

There was not the usual conventional context with which to compare the module as the Enterprise in Higher Education scheme at Wolverhampton Polytechnic had resulted in a range of innovations, mainly focussing on the development of transferable skills. However, the conventional way to deliver the module would have been by one lecture and one small group seminar a week, assessed by essays and an exam. One parallel Law module (Law, Justice and Society) used a conventional format and was used for comparison. The Business Law module was new, and so there is no comparative data from before the innovation was introduced.

These students' responses, in interviews, indicated a clear surface approach to lectures, reading and revision on the parallel Law module, reflected in their 'Reproducing' scores on the Approaches to Studying questionnaire.

> 'It is all writing down and we don't have much time for discussion...
> it's mostly dictation. You can't possibly think about what is being said.
> It is just a question of trying to decipher it later on'
> (Student's Reproducing score = 20).

The following student described her reaction to the lectures at the start of the semester:

> 'Sometimes you are having to write that fast that you switch off while you are just writing. That is what happened to me yesterday... if you are just doing dictation, because it is new you are trying to write it all down for fear of missing something.'

By the end nothing had changed:

> 'I think it is pretty much the same as when I spoke to you before... it is written down at speed and it does not really register... you do not think about it. You just write it down and you do not think about it.'

Other students described the same kind of experience:

> 'It was the only module which was straight lecture... you had two hours, two and a half hours straight lecturing just writing down, very little discussion. We had a choice. We could either listen and make points as we went along or just write furiously and hope for the best and I think we all chose to write furiously. Come revision I got all my notes and just read the notes I had made and hoped for the best, but how I passed I don't know, I really don't.'
> (Student's Reproducing score = 20).

> Student: 'They have given us a book guide. I think there is a book on the list discussing Marx. I'll probably read the minimum amount necessary... read the introduction and conclusion and skim through the bits in between.'

The following student revealed an extreme surface approach, low motivation and a very low deep approach on the Approaches to Studying questionnaire.

Achieving	Reproducing	Meaning
6	21	6

In an interview he described a surface approach to lectures and also to subsequent studying and implied a surface approach to exams as well.

'Well basically it was dictation... we just sit there and (the lecturer) just reads through his notes, we make our notes and just take it from there ... Ideally you are meant to use your lecture notes as a starting point. In an ideal world you would go off to the library and pick up the books on the booklist. Unfortunately it is not an ideal world.'

Interviewer: 'Where are you getting your understanding from?'
Student: 'Well from the lecture notes. You know, I'll read through those and pick up the sort of things they're looking for and then go through... like we have got a few headings of writers here... the broad outline... and through the exam I ought to be able to put that into the question.'

This student scored 60 percent on his essay and after the exam gained the third highest grade overall on the module, so his approach to studying was successful. The assessment on such conventional modules is not intended to encourage a surface approach, but it nevertheless both induces a surface approach and rewards or at least tolerates the quality of learning which derives from a surface approach. On this module there was a significant positive correlation between the extent to which students took a surface approach (their 'Reproducing' scores) and their assessment performance ($r = +.36$, $p < .01$). In other words the greater the extent to which students tried to reproduce material, the higher marks they obtained.

The innovation

Instead of using lectures and exams, the Business Law module used an independent learning strategy. The students were put into learning groups for the duration of the module and set six projects to undertake. Class contact of three hours a week was used to support the development and functioning of the groups, to brief students about the projects, to review the group tasks, to share learning across the groups and to develop research skills. While very short lectures were used to introduce new topics to be addressed in the projects, almost all the content of the module had to be collected by the students themselves. Assessment was 100 percent modulework. Student groups each submitted a project report for each project. The first was commented on to give formative feedback to the students and the other five were marked. Two of these were designated for the purpose of assessment for the module. There was no exam. Students discussed amongst themselves the extent to which individuals in their group had contributed to their report, and moderated each other's marks to a limited extent in a peer assessment exercise.

The following list of the projects illustrates their applied, 'real world' nature:

Project 1 A series of short questions and tasks to establish co-operative group work and identify the nature and uses of legal source material. Questions include: *'Obtain a street map of Wolverhampton and the 1990 Yellow Pages. Plot the location of Solicitors on the map. What conclusions can you draw?'*

Project 2 The design and construction of a computerised legal advice giver, accompanied by a detailed written analysis of the area of law concerned.

Project 3 The production of a report explaining the rules relating to the formation of registered companies.

Project 4 An analysis of media stories with a Business Law dimension in which each group monitored a newspaper and analysed, researched and explained the legal rules involved.

Project 5 The design and administration of a questionnaire to evaluate public knowledge of an area of law relevant to consumers and entrepreneurs.

Project 6 An interview with an individual concerned with problems in the area of Business Law, and the preparation and presentation to the individual of a report analysing the relevant law and proposing a legal resolution to the problem.

Project 3 is outlined to illustrate the extent of structure and guidance involved. This outline is drawn from a 36–page manual which supported the module.

Business Law, Task 3

Objectives

To produce a report for distribution to newly-appointed civil servants within the Department of Trade and Industry explaining the law relating to the formation of companies. Copies of appropriate forms should be obtained.

The report should make reference to the purchase of 'off the shelf' companies, and explain the advantages they offer to entrepreneurs, the costs involved and where they may be obtained from.

The report should have a section containing statistical data relating to the number of company formations and dissolutions in the period 1980–1988.

Reference will be expected to the question of a company's name, types of companies, pre-incorporation contracts, memorandum and articles of association, and the financing of companies.

The report is to be handwritten, as if for submission to a typist. A copy must be retained by each group member. Any diagrams to be included in the report should also be incorporated. There should be clear written instructions for the typist appended to the front of the report.

Skills: Group interaction, communication, use of legal resources, numeracy, time management.

Resources: Polytechnic libraries, Companies House, textbook, Central Statistical Office, Business Names Act 1985, Companies Act 1985, Companies Act 1989, Department of Trade and Industry.

Assessment: This task will be subject to a two-way assessment. Seventy-five percent of the final grade will be determined by the module leader, 25 percent by the group through the process of group assessment. The following grids will be used in respect of both types of assessment.

A list of seven criteria used by the module leader, each with a five-point rating scale, was followed by a peer assessment sheet.

Name/Group ....

Criteria	Weak			Strong	
1 Ability to work with others	1	2	3	4	5
2 Commitment to task	1	2	3	4	5
3 Ability to communicate ideas	1	2	3	4	5
4 Quality of ideas	1	2	3	4	5
5 Contribution to project	1	2	3	4	5
6 Time management	1	2	3	4	5

You may add other criteria to the above list, subject to agreement within the group and consultation with the module leader.

You must express each individual's score as a percentage.

The **average** mark within your group must be in the range 50 percent–60 percent. It is not permissible to allocate the same mark to all group members.

A completed grid for each group member must be submitted with other elements of the task on 26.4 91. Also to be submitted on this date is the logbook of one group member—to be identified in class on 25.4.91.

Students also kept a 'diary/logbook' recording work they had done, meetings with other group members, problems encountered and their resolution. This was inspected periodically by the module leader in order to monitor group's progress. The manual for the module contained an example of entries in a logbook to show students the kinds of writing expected, for example:

Week 1, Monday 28.01.91
'First task explained. Discussed it amongst the group. Seems rather difficult. None of us know anything about Company Law. Decide to make the best of it. Task divided up into elements: Damien to find statistical information and newspaper stories. Susan to find out how PRESTEL works. Richard to find out about law on insolvency, and numbers of insolvency practitioners in West Midlands. Self to find out about Company formation and report formats.

Decided to meet at lunchtime (13.00–14.00) on Thursday to discuss progress. Used staff phone to book the Art and Law Library meeting room.'

The degree of independence of these students was marked compared with the kinds of passive and superficial response to the parallel Law module described above.

For example this extract from a logbook illustrates the range of information sources students exploited and the lengths they went to in order to find things out.

> '12.3.91 Bought The Express and Star...found a range of legal topics, but one that interested me was the death of a woman when doors in a Do-It-Yourself store were not securely placed. Does it relate to Health and Safety at Work or the Tort of negligence? Anyway the court case is tomorrow at 10.00am...I think I'll appear to see whether the action will be brought in under negligence or under a breach of a condition of the Health and Safety at Work.
> 13.3.91 Appeared at the Court...
> 3.4.91 Used facilities in Central Lending Library and travelled to DTI in London, various Banks and Business Enterprise Schemes to gather information on the next task.
> 18.4.91 After the lesson the group went to a small business centre for information on companies. We also went to a business centre in Lichfield Passage.'

The class contact involved two-hour sessions once a week. The sessions involved experiential games concerning team work and interpersonal and communication skills as well as tasks, discussion and short lectures concerned with law. This mixture of teaching processes is illustrated in the Agenda for week five:

> 'The Waiting Game
> Group game (Johari's window)
> Opportunity to see and evaluate work of other groups on task 2
> Discussion of experience of peer group assessment
> Group exercise based on material covered in week 4
> Business contracts:
>   Sale of Goods
>   Trade descriptions
> Planning meeting for groups.'

The key features of this module which were intended to foster a deep approach were:

- The use of engaging projects presented in a way which generated a need to find out, rather then the presentation of information. This was intended to improve motivation.

- Active learning through project work and through task-based classroom sessions rather than lectures.

- Interaction through the use of project groups and through interactive classroom sessions.

- A well structured knowledge-base through the application of concepts to real world problems and tasks which made sense to the students.

The innovation also involved the development of students' study and research skills, the use of assessment methods and assessment criteria congruent with the aims of the module, considerable independence for first year students in the way the projects were undertaken and in the peer assessment procedure, and the use of well thought out signposts, in the manual, to a wide range of learning resources beyond the library.

The study

Students were interviewed and their logbooks examined on both the first and second operation of the module. The Approaches to Studying questionnaire was administered at the beginning and of the module on both occasions. Students on the parallel Law module were also interviewed and the Approaches to Studying questionnaire administered at the beginning and end.

The comparison between students' approach on the second operation of the module and on the parallel Law module can be seen in Table 12.1.

	Achieving	Reproducing	Meaning
Business Law (start) (n = 20)	17.91	14.91	16.36
Business Law (end)	17.32	12.37	18.37
Parallel Law (start)	13.50	14.36	15.93
(n = 19)			
Parallel Law (end)	13.32	14.31	16.37

Table 12.1: A comparison of students' approaches

By the end of the semester students on the Business Law module scored higher on the Achieving scale ($p < .001$), lower on the Reproducing scale ($p < .01$) and higher on the Meaning scale ($p < .01$) than did students on the parallel Law module. By the end of the semester on the Business Law module students had lower Reproducing scores and higher Meaning scores than at the start ($p < .01$ in each case) whereas on the parallel Law module there was no change in students' approach by the end. In other words students on the Business Law module improved on all three indicators while the students on the parallel module did not.

This improved quality of learning was evident in both students' logbooks and in their interviews.

'...the way the assignments are done you have to understand it in order to be able to do it really. Because it's not like an essay title, it is put in a different form. So really you have to understand it, because you have also got to have the information and then apply it to what the assignment is asking for—it's not just a plain essay.'

'Well it has been much better really. If you stood up there and told us parrot fashion it would be boring. It is much more interesting and if you have got a specific task, like you have related it to a something specific you learn more...you understand it better...'

The above student's Approaches to Studying scores at the end of the semester reflect her statement:

Achieving	Reproducing	Meaning
17	15	23

Students compared the experience on other modules of being told about a topic and then being asked to do more work on that topic, with their experience on Business Law of going straight into a topic with little or no preparation. They appreciated the challenge even though they found it hard work.

'You do not say "go away and read this and then do an assignment about it". You give us something to do which we have not done before, make us go and find out about it. I know that's harder to do but at the end of it when you've done it you feel much better because you feel you've achieved so much more... with other assignments you feel like you're not as interested in it because you think you have done it before, you've covered it before. It makes you do more. It's harder.'

The above student's approach, and especially his motivation, is reflected in his scores on the Approaches to Studying questionnaire.

Achieving	Reproducing	Meaning
19	13	21

The increased amount of independent reading and research was attributed by some to the nature of the class sessions.

Student: 'I find it really interesting actually. When I get home I tend to read up on it to find out more. I like to do it. I have a couple of business law books and I read up on it. I'm quite surprised because I am not usually quite so keen on things'

Interviewer: 'How do you feel about the minimalist input in the classes?'
Student: 'I think it is quite good...it makes me go away and read up on it so I know some more about it. Whereas if I got, if someone gave me all of it then I would probably not go away and read it and find it. It makes me work more for myself.'
(Student's Meaning score = 20)

Students frequently contrasted learning on the Business Law module with learning on other modules:

'Lectures we all sit down and copy lots of notes. We were actually participating and that makes it easier, makes it easier to remember.'
Interviewer: 'What is different about the way you study on this module as compared to others?'
Student: 'You know with this module it is all assessment whereas the other modules that I am taking it is all exams and the contrast that I have noticed is that with this module I am not only knowing the law but being aware and you can apply it also—if you go around and do research work, do something on your own. Whereas on the other modules after the exam I completely forgot everything.'
(Student's Meaning score = 22).

It is often assumed that students will not work independently and that if you were to reduce class contact then students will study less. The opposite appears to have been the case here. The workload on the module was quite heavy. Projects were assessed and there were no other assessment elements and so students could not avoid doing independent work. According to their logs they spent an average of 153 hours on the module (with a range of 94 hours–268 hours) on a module planned as 150 hours work. They noticed that it involved more work than their other modules.

'I have done more studying for this module I think than for anything else, I think because of the tasks (the projects). With four people there is quite a lot of work to do. So I think I put quite a lot of effort into the module. Some modules, I do seven hours of class a week anyway so obviously at home I will not devote much time to that, whereas Business Law is only three hours.'

This student compared Business Law with an Economics module:

Interviewer: 'How much time does your logbook show you have devoted to it?'
Student: 'Over 10 hours a week. For Economics I must admit I have not put in the 10 hours a week. Most of that would come down to background reading really which I have not done.'

Keeping a logbook which recorded exactly what studying had been undertaken had an impact on students' study patterns, as did the demands of the projects.

> '(before) it was a lot of spoon feeding and you were expected to go off and do work on your own, but it was never set, so people did not. But with this you think "I have not done much today" so you think you had better do some, particularly as you were keeping a logbook showing what you had done.'
> Interviewer: 'The logbook had that kind of impact on you?'
> Student: 'Yes... I was really diligent. I wrote every single thing down, exactly the time I started, exactly the time I finished...'

It is easy in conventional modules for students to do relatively little during the module and then put lots of time in revising before the exam. It is not always easy to see what is being revised, if little work has been done before, except taking and reading lecture notes, and this is exactly what students described doing on other modules. In contrast students on the Business Law module clearly undertook extensive independent work and valued the independence. The following student's Reproducing score declined from 19 to 8 during the module.

> Interviewer: 'How did you feel about the onus being on you as students to acquire knowledge?'
> Student: 'I think it is quite good because I mean when you have to leave the Polytechnic you are not going to be spoon fed are you? So you have got to be able to go off and do things on your own. So it does help you for the rest of your life.'

Students' logbooks were a rich source of evidence of the way they studied. Students showed a lot of initiative and exploited a wide range of information sources, for example:

> '10.4.91 Companies House was open so I asked for the forms needed to form a company. When I got home I phoned mum's solicitor to make an appointment to have a chat about the task to see if he could help me. 17.4.91 Had an appointment with the solicitor. He gave me some old versions of the memorandum and articles of association but they weren't much use as they were out of date. He explained about off-the-shelf companies and told me that the company he uses is called Jordans. When I got home I rang Jordans and asked them to send me some information about the kind of service they offer.'

Students were often motivated by a personal desire to understand law relevant to their own experience, for example:

> '26.10.90 Interesting to see in which areas my former employer could be prosecuted over. After studying these chapters I know enough not to be

put off or conned by an employer in the event of an accident at work. This fact is enough to make the entire module worthwhile...'

The groups were a dominant feature of students' experience:

'The fact that we were in a group was quite good because everyone had different ideas. If you had been on your own I think that would have been too much really to take on your own. Because everyone had different ideas you could egg each other on and take the best of each other.'

The following extract is from a student's logbook:

'24.4.91 It was a very long afternoon's work but we all worked very well together. There was so much legal notes relating to the assignment and it takes a very long time to search through the books etc. to find the necessary information.
24.4 91 We took great care this time to prepare our assignment and made sure that we had covered every aspect of the assignment. We worked well as a group to produce a good assignment.'

Students had sometimes experienced group work on other modules which had not worked. The reasons they identified for it working here were that time and effort was put in to team skill and the peer assessment of contributions to team work.

'My group were really good. But (another) module I have been doing has been group work and some of it has been a nightmare because you get people who do not turn up or do no work and they get the same mark as you. It does not happen in this module because of the peer group assessment. I have had trouble with all the other groups except this one.'

The positive impression given in the interviews was backed up by students' responses to a standard module evaluation questionnaire used to monitor modules. Eighty percent of students thought the module guide and reading list gave adequate background information. Ninety-five percent found the material in the module interesting. Eighty percent thought that the module was taught in an interesting and relevant manner. Ninety percent thought the staff were keen to allow questions and debate. Eighty percent thought the standard of work required was well explained and 90 percent thought that the assignments covered relevant material in the module. Ninety-five percent thought that the material covered in the module would be useful in the future. The only indifferent ratings concerned the amount of material and the length of the assignments where a substantial minority of students thought the module too demanding.

Fine-tuning

The first time the module ran, in the first semester, the results were not so encouraging as when it was repeated in the second semester, as highlighted by the results from the Approaches to Studying questionnaire. By the end of the semester, students on the first operation of the module had significantly lower Achieving scores ($p < .01$), significantly higher Reproducing scores ($p < .001$) and significantly lower Meaning scores ($p < .01$) than did students at the end of the second operation of the module. A number of problem were identified which could have led to these disappointing results:

- short multiple choice question progress tests were used and these seem to have had the effect of focussing students' attention on memorising information for the tests instead of understanding material for the projects;

- groups involved eight students. Given the students' lack of group work skills these groups were too large and resulted in some students becoming disengaged;

- in the absence of lectures a textbook was adopted. This seemed to have the effect of narrowing students' research to the textbook;

- not all students used the class time effectively;

- students felt overloaded with six projects to complete.

As a result a number of changes were introduced to address these problems:

- the progress checks were abandoned. Students logbooks were examined to obtain information about progress;

- the textbook was abandoned and students encouraged to use a wider range of sources. More detailed exercises were introduced to introduce students to the use of the law library;

- group size was reduced from eight to four and class exercises introduced to develop group skills and organisation skills in order to cope with the projects.

That all three indicators on the Approaches To Studying Questionnaire improved suggests that these were appropriate and effective changes. This illustrates the importance of fine tuning in obtaining the best results from innovations—group project work on its own did not produce the desired effects until problems were ironed out. In this case, several of the problems were caused by incongruent components of the module orienting students in the opposite direction to the main elements of the innovation.

Learning outcomes

Students' individual grades were correlated with their scores on the Approaches to Studying questionnaire. There was a significant positive correlation between students' Meaning scores and their grades ($r = +.53$, $p < .01$) but no significant correlation between either Reproducing or Achieving scores and grades. Neither the proportion of class sessions attended nor the total number of study hours recorded in students' logbooks correlated significantly with grades. In other words the only predictor of students' performance was the extent to which they took a deep approach. This contrasts with the parallel Law module in which there was a significant positive correlation between the extent of students' surface approach and their grades.

The quality of one of the students' reports was examined using the SOLO taxonomy. The meaning of the SOLO categories was defined for the fourth project students undertook and the group reports categorised using these definitions. Table 12.2 shows how student groups' mean scores on the Meaning scale were related to the SOLO level of their reports, and to their grades, the first time the module ran in semester 1. The groups are ranked in order of the grades they received. Data was only available for all three measures for the groups included in this table. The grades were on a scale of 1 to 20 where 1 is the top score. These numerical grades corresponded to letter grades of A to F, where A is the top grade.

Group (1)	Meaning scale score	SOLO level	Project 4 grade (2)	
A	15.75	2	13	(E)
B	14.25	3	11	(D)
C	16.00	3	8	(C)
E	17.50	4	6	(B)
D	19.75	5	5.5	(B)

Table 12.2: Meaning scale scores of students groups, and SOLO level and grades for project 4, in semester 1

The ranking of these three measures is identical for the five groups, with the exception of the Meaning scale score of group A. The same analysis was applied to the same project the second time the module ran and the results summarised in Table 12.3.

Again there was a very similar ranking for the grades and the SOLO level of reports, and similar rankings for group's average Meaning scores and the SOLO level of their reports, with the exception of group E.

There is too little data in these two tables to make firm conclusions. However, they suggest grades were related to the quality of reports, as indicated by their SOLO level, and that students whose groups, on average, took a deep approach to a greater extent were more likely to produce reports of a higher quality, in terms of the SOLO taxonomy, and to receive better grades. Such a pattern of relationships would have been unlikely in the parallel Law module in which students taking a surface approach did well.

Further developments

The innovator has run staff development workshops for Wolverhampton Polytechnic's Professional Development Programme, for the BA Economics module team, and for the School of Legal Studies on his innovations, as well as at regional and national conferences. A paper concerning improving student learning was circulated and was influential in the design of 17 modules validated in 1991. The Approaches to Studying Questionnaire has been adopted as a device to evaluate modules. Two new modules have been introduced, one a project work module and one a work placement module, both of which place responsibility for learning on students and involve reflection on what has been achieved by the students.

Conclusions

This module led to a quality of student learning which was markedly different from the parallel conventional Law module used for comparison. Students took a deep approach to a greater extent, a surface approach to a lesser extent and were much more motivated. Their approach improved further as the module progressed, whereas on the parallel module there was no change in students' approach. Students who took a deep approach did well, whereas on the parallel module students who took a surface approach did well. The group work operated effectively and enabled students to undertake large difficult projects on topics completely new to them. They would almost certainly not have been able to undertake tasks of such size and sophistication alone. Group work did not function so effectively on parallel modules. Students worked hard, putting in more hours than on parallel modules. Students used a wide variety of information sources, in contrast to reading on the parallel Law module.

Group	Meaning scale score	SOLO level	Project 4 grade	
C	17.50	2	13	(E)
D	17.00	3	12	(D)
G	18.00	2	10	(D)
H	19.33	4	9	(C)
F	19.75	4	6	(B)
E	17.80	5	5	(B)

Table 12.3: Meaning scale scores of students groups, and SOLO level and grades for project 4, in semester 2

These benefits were not all evident the first time the module ran, and a number of changes had to be introduced to gain the full benefits of the independent group work. The characteristics of this module which made it work, where other innovations might have failed, seem to be:

- careful attention to the building and development of effective groups, supported by an assessment mechanism—peer assessment of contributions to group work—which avoided some of the potential pitfalls;

- careful framing of the projects, with detailed attention to the resources required, the assessment criteria to be used and the relevance of the project work to the topics and to students' own interests;

- a congruent assessment system involving assessment of the projects and no other distracting elements;

- interactive class sessions which modelled the kinds of learning required and provided sufficient structure and information to launch the project work without making students passive;

- careful evaluation and diagnosis of problems and a willingness to change features which were not helping.

This case study illustrates the way a fairly complex and multifaceted course design has been introduced and tuned up until it could be shown to be producing the quality of learning intended. The departmental and institutional context supported innovation, allowed a considerable degree of autonomy in course design, allowed modifications to be made immediately, including modifications to the assessment, and exploited developments quickly in other courses and through new modules. This was a very different context to that described in Chapter 9.

Chapter 13

Improving the learning of mature students on a Certificate in Trade Union and Labour Studies

Innovator: Ewan Knox, Newcastle Polytechnic

This case study describes the way a part-time course for trade union representatives operated. It was designed to develop a range of learning skills as well as to develop understanding of trade union and labour studies. The course successfully inculcated a deep approach and students attributed this to the use of workbooks and small group discussion.

The context

Trade Union education in Britain has a long and varied tradition amongst individual unions. Since the mid 1960's moves were made to create a centralised education provision under the auspices of the Trade Union Congress. A core programme of day release provision was introduced to provide training for shop stewards and, additionally, health and safety representatives. The constraints of time and the priority of dealing with workplace issues ensured that an overall emphasis was based on training and skills development. It is widely recognised that the scheme has been successful in training many thousands of workplace representatives.

But whilst the training has been successful it was increasingly recognised that in the area of knowledge, conceptual learning and provision for educational development at higher level, a gap had emerged. Newcastle Polytechnic is a participant in the

Trade Union Congress day release scheme for trade union representatives. It was one of a number of institutions which have attempted to bridge the gap and to meet the aspirations of trade unions and trade unionists for educational opportunities. A CNAA Certificate in Trade Union and Labour Studies started in January 1990 with 32 students. The part-time nature of the course is important in allowing students to remain within their communities, taking advantage of higher-level study without risk of financial sacrifice associated with full-time education. The course has recruited two further intakes in January 1991 and October 1991.

The overall course aim is to provide active trade unionists with the opportunity to improve their education and qualifications and follow studies relevant to their work and Labour Movement experiences. The principle objectives to the course are:

- To provide advanced education in trade union and labour studies both theoretical and practical.

- To provide possible pathways for those wishing to continue on to other courses up to degree level and beyond.

- To provide an introduction for graduates to the theory and practice of industrial relations.

The course objectives are divided into three sections, two of which are concerned with processes rather than content:

b) Skills.
   The students will be given the opportunity to develop:

   (i) Analytical skills and conceptual understanding.

   (ii) Identifying and using appropriate sources of information.

   (iii) Using appropriate techniques and methods to collect information.

   (iv) Sifting, classifying and interpreting information.

   (v) Thinking logically and systematically.

   (vi) Critically analysing issues and problems.

   (vii) Interpreting and applying concepts to practical situations.

c) Communication Skills The students will be given the opportunity to develop their:

   (i) Ability to argue coherently and logically in written form.

   (ii) Ability to manage discussions with people.

   (iii) Ability to communicate information to people in a variety of ways.

149

(iv) Ability to encourage and develop participation both individually and in a group context.

The course is two years part-time and involves one evening per week and nine Saturday mornings per year. In addition there is a certain amount of distance learning in each subject. The way student learning hours are distributed is summarised in Table 13.1.

Subject	Lectures & Seminars	Saturdays	Group Work, Tutorials	Distance Learning
Study Skills	9	0	0	5
Research Skills	9	3	2	5
Labour History	12	6	2	8
Trade Unions, Management of IR	22	6	5	13
Understanding Society	9	3	2	5
Politics	18	6	3	10
Economics	21	6	5	12
Inequality at Work	12	3	3	8
Internationalism	9	3	2	5
Work, New Technology & Society	12	6	3	8
Psychology of IR	12	3	3	8
Labour and the Law	12	6	3	8
Micro Studies	18	3	3	0
Total	175	54	36	95

Table 13.1: Distribution of student hours

Evenings usually contain three sessions: two for lectures or seminars and one shorter session in the middle of the evening for tutorials on distance learning. Each component of the course has a set amount of distance learning work allotted to it. This is separate from the course assignments, and is not assessed. It takes the form of guided reading, comprehension, preparation for future seminars, workplace reports and progress checks. In the middle period of the evening session students may engage in group tutorials in which the distance learning work is collectively discussed and learning difficulties identified. The session is also be used to provide individual feedback on assignments and to support the identification of individual learning needs.

Teaching Methods

The recruitment of largely mature students with mixed ability backgrounds to the course means that teaching methods have to be selected with care. The long-standing involvement of members of the teaching team in adult education, particularly through trade union courses, is important here. Each lecturer gears the content of their own particular course towards the specific needs of mixed ability students but a number of general approaches have been adopted.

1. The course draws no rigid demarcation between lectures and seminars. Each teaching session is flexible enough to include knowledge-based inputs from teaching staff coupled with student participation. This may take a number of forms including open forums, small group activities, case studies and student presentations. In this way the level at which the content is addressed can be set by staff, whilst students can relate their own experience and understanding to the ideas being explored. An example of this approach is given below.

2. Materials have been developed which cover more than one specific area. For example, a case study of the 1984/5 miners' strike offers opportunities to integrate teaching in politics, economics, labour law, gender and labour history.

3. The distance learning element of the course provides the opportunity for some self-paced learning. This work is backed up by staff tutorial support. The Certificate Course in Trade Union and Labour Studies already provided by the Polytechnic in conjunction with the TGWU on a distance learning basis has a printed teaching pack of almost 200 pages alongside three activities booklets and this provides the basis for teaching programmes on this course.

4. Regular three-hour Saturday morning teaching periods provide a further opportunity to develop student-based learning on specific subject areas.

5. There is built in personal tutorial support of 20 hours over each year.

A sample session

The closed shop is an issue on which most students have some direct knowledge as well as their own opinions. It is likely that they will lack any general perspective on the closed shop as an institution or will have thought critically about it from either a trade union or management perspective. It is also unlikely that they will have a rigorous understanding of the legal framework involved. A teaching session on the closed shop might take the form shown in Table 13.2.

The key features of the course which are designed to foster a deep approach are:

- the nature of the evening sessions, which stress interaction

- problem-based tasks for individuals and groups

- the link between students' experience and new material to help provide a well structured knowledge base

- the use of project work to encourage active learning. A project forms a major component of the assessment.

The Closed Shop: Session Outline

1. A lecture giving a factual account of the development, extent and types of closed shop agreements

2. Discussions of students' own closed shop arrangements, or lack of them, undertaken in groups of five or six.

3. A small group activity to look at the advantages and disadvantages of the closed shop to both trade unionists and management.

4. A lecture on the legal framework.

5. A linked forum discussion on the role of law.

Table 13.2: An example teaching session

- the development of learning skills and research skills through classroom exercises and group and distance learning. A total of 33 hours is allocated to this work: almost 10 percent of the course.

- support for the development of independent learning, including choice of essays and the opportunity to negotiate alternative forms of assignments.

Assessment

The course is assessed by a series of essays and by a project in the second year. These assignments are relatively conventional in nature but are used in order to prepare students for conventional higher education courses which many wish to go to.

Problems

The course team were in the main from backgrounds in adult education and were committed to student centred-learning and the encouragement of individual and independent learning. They were also convinced of the value of small group discussion in fostering a deep approach to learning. However, while the students had plenty of experience, and strong opinions to express, they often lacked the knowledge to make discussion productive.

The diagnosis of the situation was that motivational context, learner activity and interaction with others were already strong features within the course. Where development was needed was with a well structured knowledge-base. This could not be achieved simply by referring students to books because, being part-time 'return to learning' students, they had problems of access to the library and limited study skills. The course team recognised the crucial role of acquisition of concepts, understanding and critical thought. However increasing the proportion of lectures was also unlikely to solve this problem, as these extracts from students' interviews revealed:

> ' ...a lecture is a means of getting the information from the lecturer's notes to the students' notes without touching any brain in between...all that does for me is maybe give me some ideas of what to look at afterwards.'

> 'I think when you tend to be lectured at you only get one person's point of view.'

> 'The ones I hate are the ones ...where you are lectured at and you mainly sit there scribbling notes down and looking at things on overhead projectors.'

Instead they decided to produce what they called 'workbooks'—packs containing a range materials providing a wide range of perspectives on a topic. One of the main foci of interviews with students was on the use of workbooks in Trade Unionism and Internationalism. Internationalism was chosen as the topic for the innovation because of its inaccessibility as a topic, with reading material dispersed and often difficult to come by.

Workbooks

In designing the workbooks an emphasis was placed on developing a conceptual understanding and framework from which to interpret change in a global context. The workbooks dealt with key concepts of interpretation, analysis and methodologies. They provided reading material and guidance on further reading. They were used to enable checks on progress to be made, to give groups tasks to undertake, and to enable students to undertake study away from the Polytechnic. The materials consisted of two elements.

1. Four volumes of readings covering specific themes: colonialism, imperialism and global capitalism; the development of the transnational corporation; labour and the transnationals; Europe, economic transformation, labour and the unions. It was agreed by the core staff on the course that the overall emphasis should be placed on understanding colonialism as an economic and political system rather than its effects or legacy—on the conceptual rather than the factual.

2. A series of activities designed to promote small group discussion and a series of progress checks for individual study.

Students use of the workbooks was integrated into the course by requiring individual students to read part of the workbook and to contribute to a small group discussion on the basis of this reading by preparing and presenting short deliveries on various aspects of the subject. Small group discussion exercises were then followed by a wider discussion with the whole group, coordinated by a tutor, and a summary.

In the notes accompanying the materials students were informed of their uses (Table 13.3).

The study

The study involved the administration of the Approaches to Studying questionnaire at the start and end of the Internationalism course, in the 2nd year, and also with 1st year students. A sample of 20 percent of students were also interviewed at the start and end of the Internationalism course.

From the Approaches To Studying questionnaire data it can be seen that students were taking a surface approach to a lesser extent, at the start of the second year 'Internationalism' course than did 1st year students ($p < .01$) though their Achieving and Meaning scores were not significantly different to those of first year students. Their Reproducing scale scores were already low and their Meaning scale scores already extraordinarily high by the start of this second year course. By the end of the Internationalism course students took a deep approach to a significantly greater extent ($p < .01$) and were significantly more motivated to achieve ($p < .01$). In addition, and this needs some explanation, they were also adopting a surface approach to a significantly greater extent ($p < .01$)—at about the level of the average for social science students.

It was easy to identify students' conception of learning, underlying their deep approach, in their interviews.

> Interviewer: 'What does the word education mean to you?'
> Student: 'I would have thought education means something other than it meant to me when I first started the course. Education, going to school, learning by rote, that's not education at all. That's simply getting paid to channel children's minds, to stop them using their imagination. You're not bringing out their intelligence. Education to me should be that you stimulate, you get people to question, because you can't make somebody learn something if they don't want to learn. So education should mean getting people to question, to open people's minds...'
> Interviewer: 'What importance would you place on memorising information?'
> Student: 'Well, memorising 1066 and all that sort of stuff is pretty useless because it doesn't give you any understanding of the issues. But I think if you are talking about learning notes I've not had to do that as such. But I think if you have a basic understanding of what it's all about you remember it anyway.'

Aims of the Workbooks

- To provide a ready source of written material on historical and contemporary aspects of internationalism and how it relates to the labour movement.

- To develop your conceptual understanding and awareness of the importance of global factors facing the labour movement.

Notes on the use of workbooks
The workbooks for this part of the course are an aid to learning and are not a substitute for your own wider reading. The workbooks will be used on three levels. Firstly you will find that they can be used to work at your own pace and you will find a number of progress checks for this purpose accompanying each section. Secondly they will be used for discussion-based learning in groups. Here you will find a number of discussion-based activities that accompany particular sections.Thirdly, particular focus will be placed on understanding many of the concepts that allow us to interpret and analyse world events.

Progress checks
These take the form of short written assignments undertaken on a group or individual basis where you are asked perhaps to define concepts which help us to understand society and social relationships within society, or you may be asked to prepare an account of a particular institution or event. Done to the best of your ability this will pay its own dividends in the understanding and interpreting of issues and events. Progress checks will also form the basis of open class discussion.

Discussion Activity
There are discussion activities in the workbook which ask you to look at aspects of issues with other members of the group. Here your knowledge and experience is a crucial factor in the discussion progress. Remember we learn more by talking issues through to clarify points, concepts, etc. than by simply accumulating facts or a store of knowledge.

Things to Do
Some activities may ask you to undertake research on an issues either to find information from your workplace, union, library or other places.

Table 13.3: Notes accompanying the workbooks

	Achieving	Reproducing	Meaning
Start of 'Internationalism'	12.45	11.45	18.81
End of 'Internationalism'	14.50	13.40	20.50
1st year students	13.70	15.00	18.90
Social Science norms	12.73	13.65	14.21

Table 13.4: Mean scores on the Approaches to Studying questionnaire

The role of discussion in fostering a deep approach was clear in what students said:

'Well I'm not learning by rote. I think it's a result of this course. I came on this course and you can get something out of it—you don't have to sit and listen to this person at the front telling you things. You can actually ask questions, participate.'

'It comes back to participating in your own education. Because it is all too easy to sit at the back and do nothing. But if you are given a specific thing to do for next week...doing extra reading ... you can actually join in. I think this is very important on this course that people do join in, that it's not the kind of course where you can be passive.'

'It was a two-way thing—there was lots of debate. In a class of twenty there was lots of different opinions. Whereas when someone is just standing talking to you you never understand...I think it's a much better process.'

'It's principally...talking to other people about it like friends, because you have got to have someone to bounce ideas off.'

'You find that some people who are very quiet actually have very interesting ideas on things that you wouldn't get from a larger group. If you can split it into smaller groups and then let it come back to a big discussion...this is much more enjoyable than just getting fed facts. I think it is because I like talking more than I like listening. I suppose it comes back to school days when all you could do was listen to what the teacher said without questioning it. It has a soporific effect on me. I just drift.'

'I've really enjoyed the course...when we're in small groups I can put my opinions across and I feel more confident in what I'm actually saying and as it turns out it's changed my whole outlook on life.'

Students also recognised that it wasn't 'joining in' on its own, which brought the benefits. They criticised other, less structures sessions. The structure imposed by the way the reading of the workbooks was shared round and the way the sessions were structured, was crucial to the quality of the discussion.

> '(He) tended to let things get out of hand. Certain people did appear to dominate. There didn't appear to be any great structure. There were occasions when I was confused as to what he wanted... the Politics course was very participatory but it didn't seem to get anywhere. Internationalism was very participatory and it did get a long way.'

> 'I think it seemed that the discussions were a lot more concise than the sort of wide messy bunfights that we get into sometimes.'

> 'Sometimes discussions can be utterly useless and just people just voicing off their own opinions, and I think you can probably avoid that more by providing background information like this.'

The workbooks had a marked effect on the quality of these discussions for many students:

> Interviewer: 'If you were doing the set reading that was asked of you, did you find that useful in allowing you to contribute more to the discussion that followed the next week?'
> Student: 'Yes, it did. Because you'd read a thing from it and bits would stick in your mind, and the same would apply to anybody who had done the reading. It lead to a more structured discussion than we would have had, had we not had a chance to look at these first. A good thing about them was that everybody had them whereas if you are relying on books some people may have got the one that was on the list but others wouldn't. So it made it clearer.'
> Interviewer: 'Do you think the workbooks and the way they were used in any way improved the learning situation?'
> Student: 'I think they did... in that everybody had access to them. So it meant that people were talking from recent information they'd received rather than from something they'd found out 15 years ago or whatever. It certainly improved the class sessions... I certainly think the class sessions were more useful.'

This was contrasted with their previous experience of discussions:

> 'I think it could have been that three people might have done some work and everybody would have sat back and let them get on with it. They would have tended to dominate the discussion. If everybody has a set task you know more or less what you would be expected to discuss.'

157

The assessment criteria seemed well understood by the students. They found no difficulty in explaining what the tutors were looking for in the essays:

> Interviewer: 'In the assessment what do you think the teachers are after?'
> Student: 'Showing a level of understanding. Not so much reflecting your opinions but to show that at least you understand the subject... the ability to back up your argument with evidence and justify what you're saying.'

> 'I think you're looking to see if we gained an understanding of the subject.'

> 'I think the tutor will be looking to see if I've understood. Not that it's a trick question but there's something more behind the question, and looking for that something and getting more understanding.'

> 'I think they want to know that somebody has looked at the question and considered the options and can then... make up their mind about the topic... so it can increase their understanding... that's what learning's all about.'

Students brought their own experience into their writing and discussion a great deal:

> 'I base a lot of it on the experience I've had over a lot of years.'

They also recognised that their experience was not enough:

> 'I think first of all that it's shown me that I didn't know as much about things as I though I knew. I know my experience in the movement has come in handy on a number of things. Its awakened a desire in us to do more studying.'

The workbooks and the way students were required to use them introduced an element of rigour which had sometimes been missing before:

> 'It's got me into a disciplined way of reading. Before you can have a casual attitude. I'll watch this programme on television. I might do a bit of reading. But as the course has progressed you really had to sit down and put away your time. Like this is the time when you study.'

> 'I'm a lot more selective about the information I actually include in essays or refer to. At first I would be getting three books and reading them all whereas now I read more books and pick out little bits or particular interest or relevance and discard a lot of the information.'

> 'I suppose its taught me how to look critically at a situation instead of just accepting what a situation appears to be.'

Interviewer: 'Do you think the workbooks, allied to what you were doing in class, helped you in any way to learn more effectively?'
Student: 'I think more effectively. I have this awful tendency to wander off and with these resource packs I had a broad outline there for me. There was less chance that I would be wandering off. With some sessions I have got totally lost. With these (workbooks) you know what you have to do for the following week.'

The whole way of working on the Internationalism course, and the tutorial support, also had a marked impact on students' ability to study—both their organisation and their skills. As this was one of the main objectives of the whole course this is an achievement which should not be underestimated. To start with students were often in a lot of difficulty with their studying.

'At first I was just scribbling and reading the books—speed reading. I used the basis of notes to write the essay at the end. When I first started on this course I felt like a fish out of water'

Later on students described being much more organised, selective and purposeful in their studying.
The quantitative evidence from the Approaches to Studying questionnaire showed students to adopt a surface approach to a greater extent at the end of the course. Although students' started from initially low 'Reproducing' scores this still requires some explanation. There were several clues from the interviews. Some students felt rushed and said that the sessions were too short. Some students found it hard to put in the studying time necessary to keep up:

'I tend to stick to the reading list...I find that in the middle of shift work I do my best just to keep up with what is there.'

'...we were a bit nonplussed when we got the assignment because we hadn't had time to cover it.'

Others reported another course making inappropriate assumptions about students' prior knowledge:

'It was just like throwing you into deep water with a weight around your neck and telling you to swim...by the time he discovered that we didn't have a grounding in economics it was too late.'

Some felt that the content of the workbooks was not as relevant to the content of the course as they might have been:

'They didn't seem particularly to cover what we were covering on the course week by week. Sometimes they had a vague relevance...some of the later ones didn't have much relevance to what we were doing at the time.'

Others felt that by having workbooks they read less widely than they might otherwise have done:

'It made me lazier I think for that term because of the resource books ...so I didn't use the library nearly as much as I would have done.'

Any or all of these pressures could have induced a surface approach to an extent. To avoid this possibility the course could monitor course demands for possible overloading, undertake more staff development so that tutors take more care about the level of students prior knowledge, link the design of sessions more carefully to the workbooks and link the content of the workbooks out to other sources so that students do not become too reliant on them.

Student Learning Outcomes

Students' assessment results did not show the Internationalism course to have led to significantly better marks than on other courses. Students gained an average of 65.2% as against an average of 63.5% on the other eight courses.

The qualitative evidence presented a different picture. The tutor involved recognised a difference compared with the previous year where there had been problems with the conceptual side of the course.

'The early focus on conceptual issues associated with imperialism and colonialism provided the basis for students' understanding of the later 'issue-based' subjects. I was pleased to find students returning to this earlier work in later discussions. It is worth noting that the essays have focussed on conceptual issues such as colonialism rather than what might seem to be the more 'bread and butter' issues of multi-national collective bargaining. Overall, I believe we were largely successful in developing a conceptual understanding in the students about the nature of international issues. The specific discussion of colonialism and the world economy were particularly good in that respect and informed much of the discussion throughout the course.'

Costs

The staff involved estimated the development costs of the workbooks at 100 hours of staff time or £2,000 worth of part-time replacement. The way the sessions were run would also require staff development, as would the way the materials were prepared. The staff estimated that two days training would be required for all staff involved in such a programme. Once set up the methods cost no more to run—the small group discussions taking place within a 'workshop' type session with one tutor managing the whole process.

Conclusions

The interviews highlighted the same points again and again:

- Whatever approach students took initially—and they took a surface approach to a much greater extent in their 1st year—they were taking a clear, deep approach to studying the Internationalism course, almost without exception.

- Most students were able to contrast this learning with what had taken place before: at school, on other courses, or earlier on this course.

- Discussion and active participation was crucial to most students. A few took a deep approach primarily in their private reading but for most it was joining in discussion which moulded and changed their approach.

- It was important that the discussion took place in small 'private' discussion groups rather than in the whole class, although whole class discussion was valuable once small group discussion had taken place. Whole class discussions on other course elements were criticised because they allowed individuals to dominate.

- The workbooks helped provide a common information and conceptual base which helped avoid the discussions being dominated by past experience and mere opinion. Not all students preferred reading from the workbooks, though for many the practical problems of accessing information sources in any other way were insurmountable.

- Both students and tutors recognised the improved quality of learning—both its process and its outcomes.

Chapter 14

Conclusions from the case studies

While the case studies involved a wide variety of innovations in a wide variety of contexts, a number of common features emerged. It is important to recognise that these common features would have been hard to recognise without the conceptual framework this book offers. Conclusions are summarised here with references back to the case studies which illustrate the points.

1. A surface approach is very common.

It is not the case that a surface approach is only exhibited by very poor students or on exceptionally poor courses. In these case studies a surface approach was pervasive. It might even be seen as the normal approach on conventional courses where no steps have been taken to avoid it or to foster a deep approach. Examples of a surface approach were found in every context examined by the case studies. In most of the courses used for comparison a surface approach was dominant. In some of the case studies a surface approach was still very much in evidence even after the innovation had been introduced. The qualitative evidence, from interviews with students, often gave an extremely depressing picture of the quality of learning taking place. The scale of the problem should not be underestimated.

2. Different courses reveal very different patterns of learning.

The mean surface approach scores on different courses studied here varied from about 12 to about 16 and deep approach scores from about 13 to about 19. These differences were as wide within institutions as between institutions so the institutions themselves cannot have been the main cause of variation. The differences were also wide even when the same students were involved. There were very marked differences between one year and the next for the same students and between different courses the same students were taking in parallel. So differences between student groups cannot have

162

been the main source of variation. It seems clear that the wide variations in students' approaches were due to differences between the courses.

3. Individual differences in approach are extremely wide.

In every case study there were examples of students studying the same course who took dramatically different approaches. Students working alongside each other were capable of taking extreme surface or extreme deep approaches to the same course. Interestingly when students worked in groups they were likely to adopt a common approach within the group. For example in Chapter 12 one group had a mean deep approach score of 19.75 while another had an mean score of only 14.25. There is clearly plenty of scope to influence the approach individual students take within a fixed course.

4. Students' approaches to studying can be highly volatile

Looking beyond the influence of innovations on the mean approach scores of the whole group of students it was possible to identify individuals who changed dramatically. Students sometimes switched almost completely from an extreme surface approach to an extreme deep approach. Such dramatic change is possible. It can also be quite rapid. Some students had adopted a very different approach to that they had previously adopted within a few weeks of starting the new course. Not all such dramatic changes were positive, however. For example in Chapter 5 one student's deep approach score declined from 17 to 3 as soon as she returned from her work placement and started her conventionally taught final year. There seems plenty of scope for having marked impacts on students' approaches.

5. Changes in students' approach are not due to maturation

It might be thought that inexperienced and young students would tend to adopt a surface approach and that as they matured they would learn how to adopt a deep approach. This seems to be a complete misreading of what actually happens. The highest deep approach scores encountered were from first year students and the lowest were from third year students. Where data was available on parallel courses in which there were no significant changes in teaching and learning methods (eg in Chapter 7) students' surface approach scores increased as they progressed through the course. This confirms evidence cited in Chapter 1 that students may progressively abandon a deep approach as they move through higher education. A further piece of evidence which contradicts the 'maturation' notion is that in the only case study where there were parallel conventional and mature students (in Chapter 10, where second year undergraduates undertook the same course as postgraduate Diploma students from industry) the mature students adopted a surface approach to a greater extent. Whether a student adopts a deep or a surface approach appears to have little to do with their age or extent of experience of higher education. It is the nature of that experience which matters.

6. Most students seem capable of adopting either a surface or a deep approach

Some students appeared to have such an unsophisticated conception of learning that they would be unlikely to adopt a deep approach whatever the context. The vast majority of students, however, seemed perfectly capable of taking either approach and many described taking quite a different approach on a course parallel to that being studied. There was evidence of students' growing understanding of what learning involved and what courses demanded and this may have increased the extent to which they responded to course contexts.

7. It is possible to change students' approach

This is the most important conclusion of the study. Most of the case studies demonstrated a significant positive impact on students' approaches to studying. This was evident in scores on the Approaches to Studying questionnaire and even more evident in interviews. On most occasions where this change was identified it was also possible to demonstrate that parallel courses did not induce a similar change or that previously there had been no change. Lecturers should feel quite encouraged that it is clearly possible to have significant impacts on the quality of student learning through changes in course design and teaching and learning methods.

8. It is easier to change students' approach early in a course than towards the end

It is sometimes argued that students cannot cope with innovatory methods early on in their courses and that it is better to wait until the third year before giving them projects to do or expecting any independence. The case studies demonstrate quite the opposite. The three case studies which showed least positive impact on the quality of student learning involved the final year of a course. There was clear evidence in each case that students had developed a pattern of learning and a response to course demands, through their experience of earlier parts of the course, which were going to be hard to change. A surface approach had proved sufficiently successful thus far and students were not going to take any risks messing around with a deep approach so close to finishing their course. In these cases it might have been impossible to have much of an impact whatever the innovation had consisted of and however well it had been executed. It is vital to start the process of inducing a deep approach and developing good study habits early on.

Other case studies (for example Chapters 4 and 12) showed how students can be supported in being independent and in adopting a deep approach in their first term in higher education. Students develop an understanding of what learning is, and what they should be doing when learning, from messages implicit in the way courses are designed and taught. If they are required to be passive they learn to be passive and it can be very difficult for them to unlearn this later on. The conservatism of students used to one way of learning was one of the main blocks to improving quality encountered by the project.

164

9. Intrinsic motivation is crucial

A common refrain from lecturers is that their students are not sufficiently motivated. To increase motivation they often take steps such as increasing course work demands and making testing more frequent or more threatening. In none of the case studies was students' Achieving score related to their assessment marks. The reason for this appears to be that students' motivation takes two main forms: intrinsic and extrinsic. Intrinsic motivation is concerned with interest in the subject and a desire to understand. Brophy (1986) defined motivation as: 'The tendency to find academic activities meaningfull and worthwhile and to try to get the intended academic benefits from them'. Extrinsic motivation is concerned with a desire to pass—or fear of failure. It is easy to increase extrinsic motivation through threatening assessment demands. However this also induces a surface approach. Intrinsic motivation comes from within the individual and is much harder to foster. Several of the case studies described students working very hard in an organised way in order to pass or get good marks, but doing this through an extreme surface approach. Some students were quite able to distinguish those parts of course they were learning for themselves and those parts they were learning for others—for the assessment alone.

In order to improve the quality of student learning it is not enough to increase motivation. It is neccessary to increase intrinsic motivation without increasing extrinsic motivation.

10. Assessment dominates students' thinking to a considerable extent

Students had clear views concerning how to pass their courses and what they had to to in order to gain good marks. These views were not always identical to the views of their teachers, but they dominated the way they responded to the course. Where innovations in teaching were not accompanied by congruent innovations in assessment they had the least impact (for example in Chapters 5 and 11). Even well conceived and well executed innovations are likely to fail if the assessment is unchanged and does not reinforce the implicit messages of the course concerning what is to be learned. Where new assessment methods were introduced it was crucial that their demands were made explicit through specification of criteria, briefing and discussion in order to change students' perceptions about what they ought to be aiming for.

11. Some assessment systems clearly reward a surface approach

In several case studies courses parallel to those being studied were demonstrated to give higher marks to students who took a surface approach. In contrast in several case studies, for example Chapter 12, the assessment system clearly rewarded a deep approach. In one case study, Chapter 9, different halves of the assessment rewarded different approaches. The half of the exam questions which corresponded to the half of the course involving the innovation allowed students who took a deep approach to gain higher marks, while for the other half of the exam questions, corresponding to the conventionally taught half of the course, students who took a surface approach gained higher marks.

It is vital to design your assessment system, and even details of exam questions, so that a deep approach is rewarded to a greater extent than a surface approach. It is also vital, following (9) above, that students are fully aware of what is rewarded.

12. *Successful innovations may have only local or short-lasting impacts*

Several case studies revealed how an innovation can be successfully introduced and have the intended positive impacts on student learning whilst students are studying the course concerned. However this impact can be very local, in that students may not study parallel courses in the same way. They can also be very short-lasting. In Chapters 5 and 7 students reverted to earlier, lower quality, approaches to studying as soon as they were back in conventional contexts or confronted with conventional exams. The approaches students take are extraordinarily context-dependent and it cannot be assumed that by improving one module or course element you can permanently change students.

13. *It is possible to have a pervasive impact on students*

Despite the pessimism in (11) above one case study demonstrated extensive long-term impacts on students. In the engineering course described in Chapter 7 students did not revert to their previous approach once they returned to a conventional context. They would not tolerate being taught conventionally after experiencing a problem-based course and staff were obliged to devise a different programme for them. And two years later they approached project work in a very different way than their colleagues who had been taught conventionally. What distinguished this case study and what may explain the extent of its impact is that it involved comprehensive changes in students' entire learning time for two terms rather than modifications to only one of several parallel courses students were taking.

14. *The appropriate focus of attention in improving the quality of student learning is course design and process rather than teaching and content*

Concerns about the quality of teaching in higher education are often narrowly focussed on lecturers' classroom performance. Appraisal of teaching and evaluation of courses often focusses almost exclusively on what the teacher does and especially on what the teacher does whilst lecturing. Review of courses often concentrates almost exclusively on what content is 'covered' and external scrutiny of exam questions also focusses on the 'what' rather than the 'how'. Details of the 'what' are largely missing from the case studies and descriptions of exactly how lectures were undertaken are notable by their absence. The features which seem to have been crucial to improving quality were to do with course design—with the way processes engaged students in learning. Decisions about whether to include topic A rather than topic B would have made virtually no difference to any of the cases. In contrast a decision to leave out both A and B in order to give students more time to think might well have had an impact. Similarly while many of the cases still involved lectures, the quality of these lectures was not often an issue. In Chapter 10, for example the lectures which formed part of the programme were not referred to at all by the students and the case study focussed on the influential aspects of the inovation instead. Where lectures were highlighted by students it was where they induced a surface approach. Most of the case studies used few or no lectures and in most the role of the teacher was one of organisation of learning opportunities and the support of independence rather than the presentation of material.

Focussing on what teachers do, and especially on what they do and on what they cover in lectures, is an inappropriate way of attempting to improve the quality of student learning. Even superb presentations can induce a surface approach. Instead the focus should be on what aspects of course design foster a deep approach.

15. It takes skill and fine tuning to make methods work

Despite the argument in (14) above there is still plenty of room for teaching skill to have an impact. While the conceptual framework offered in this book provides good guidance concerning what kinds of methods to introduce, it still takes skill and fine tuning to make the methods work. The methods described in Chapter 6 took years to develop and the innovation described in Chapter 12 did not produce the desired improvements in student learning the first time it ran. Not until a number of changes had been introduced the second time it ran did students' increase the extent of their deep approach. In Chapter 7 the innovation was introduced with a pilot group of only six students before being extended to a full cohort. It would have been risky to attempt such an extensive and novel innovation with a large class. In contrast Chapter 9 described an method which was new to the innovator and to the students in a very conventional context and with a large class. The innovation had to be abandoned before the methods involved had been developed enough to make them work.

Skill may take very different forms than those normally associated with good teaching, however. Instead of being concerned with lecturing, the crucial skills may involve being able to brief students appropriately for a class-based activity or independent group work, being able to design assignments which foster a deep approach, or being able to comment on reflective journals in a way which fosters further reflection. The repertoire of skills used by the innovators involved in the case studies is very different to those focussed on in most student feedback forms. The conventional assumptions of these forms threaten innovation because it is possible to be rated poorly whilst fostering high quality learning. I have encounterd lecturers who say they cannot afford to innovate due to the nature of the evaluation system used to review their performance as teachers.

16. *The conceptual framework offered here provides a powerful tool for improving the quality of learning*

The conceptual framework offered here illuminated the case studies in a way which previous evaluations had not. It offers a higher level conception of teaching which is vital for improving the quality of learning. Tobin and Fraser (1988) in a study of science and mathematics teaching found that all teachers identified as exemplary operated from a sophisticated conception of teaching and were sensitive to learning outcomes and to the learning processes students used to produce those outcomes. The research methods used in the case studies resulted in the innovators achieving a greater understanding of the learning processes going on. The engagement of lecturers in the study of their courses is crucial to the improvement of courses, but without a clear conceptual framework concerned with learning evaluation may have little positive impact. Conventional course evaluation questionnaires were used in a number of the case studies, but they added relatively little to an understanding of what was happeneing and they were not influential in convicing colleagues. In contrast evidence about the quality of learning was much more convincing. The Approaches to Studying questionnaire was adopted as a module evaluation device for a Department following its use in the Law module described in Chapter 12. Evidence from interviews and learning journals and diaries made those involved aware of what was going on in a way which conventional evaluation had not. And evidence from the use of the SOLO taxonomy revealed the quality of students' learning outcomes in a way marking had not. The SOLO taxonomy is being used to assist the assessment of clinical practice following its use in the case in Chapter 11. The case studies illustrate the way steps to improve teaching have been based on a new conception of learning.

Higher education now uses course evaluation a great deal to make decisions—about courses and about lecturers—but this evaluation has tended to have no conceptual underpinning. In evaluating teaching we must have a model of what good teaching consists of (Ramsden, 1988). This project has illustrated a way for lecturers to become engaged with reconceptualising teaching and learning in their courses and through this process to become exemplary teachers.

17. *Lecturers are perfectly capable of researching their own teaching*

Perhaps the most heartening and, in the long term, most important finding, is that educational researchers are not neccessary. The impetus for the project came from the ever widening gap between the understanding in the research literature of what quality in learning consists of, and how to foster it, on the one hand, and the unsophisticated practice of course design, teaching and evaluatuion on the other. This gap existed because the research was undertaken by researchers and the teaching, course design and evaluation was undertaken by the teachers. This division of labour is unhelpful and unneccessary. The innovators in the case studies were not educational researchers but lecturers who cared about quality, though perhaps not 'ordinary' lecturers. They needed, and received, very little support. While the improvements in student learning achieved in the case studies were heartening, the long term benefit of the project will come when others realise that they can improve their own courses through similar action research into their own teaching. The last two chapters in this book are designed to provide support for lecturers in the process of undertaking research without the help of researchers.

Chapter 15

Introducing change

It is not usually difficult to persuade lecturers that some forms of change in courses are desirable. It is much harder to persuade them that it is possible. Change can be difficult to bring about. Some of the innovations described in the case study, although deliberately selected so as not to seem too radical or too large scale to be possible to emulate, must still seem unattainable to many lecturers. Most lecturers have had little or no training in teaching or course design, let alone training in action research into their own teaching, and are not used to leading innovations and leading their colleagues. The following advice is offered to support those wishing to change. It is based in part on the experience of those involved in the case studies—both those who succeeded in changing others and those who did not—and in part on my own experience over years of trying to bring about change.

1. Find allies

In the only case study which described an innovation which had to be abandoned, in Chapter 9, the innovator had no allies at all. Isolated innovations are very vulnerable. Innovations can threaten the status quo and the values and beliefs of other lecturers and can stir up strong opposition. You need allies who understand what you are doing and why and who share your general intentions if not your methods. This is not only useful politically, it can be valuable to discuss what you are doing with someone sympathetic and also valuable to have some moral support. Allies outside your Department may be valuable for technical support—for example someone from an Educational Development Unit—but allies from within your Department are necessary politically. Seek out likely allies and bring them in on what you are doing. Ask their advice and involve them, if possible, in interviewing students or in sharing some of the teaching or assessment. Invite them to collect similar evidence about their own course so that you can compare what is going on. Whatever you do, don't go it alone.

2. Identify the problem clearly

In many of the case studies the description of the situation before the innovation was introduced, or on parallel conventional courses, was depressing enough to convince any reasonable person that change was necessary. By evaluating the situation you are wishing to change you can provide strong evidence to support your innovation. This will require the kinds of evidence collected in the case studies.

Exam results and conventional student feedback data is unlikely to back your case. Over the past ten years student numbers have soared and resources have declined and yet more students obtain first class honours degrees than ever before. No-one I have met believes that quality has improved and so it must be that the problems are being covered up, rather than exposed, by the assessment system. Similarly, damning student feedback has not, in my experience, led to radical change. It might lead to a lecturer being criticised or even moved to lecture on a different course, but not to changes in course design. This is because the evidence is in a form which, because it lacks a conceptual framework, is incapable of suggesting what else one might do other than lecture.

To highlight the need for change you need to collect evidence which is interpretable within a framework which would enable you to identify appropriate directions of change. The case studies demonstrate the collection and use of exactly this kind of evidence.

3. Use research evidence

Chapter 1 contains a summary of research evidence which many lecturers find compelling. They find that it coincides with their own experience but that in the past they have had nothing but their hunches to go on. The research evidence in this area is very robust and hangs together well to tell a coherent story which non-educationalists can make sense of. Use it to convince others. Chapter 16 contains exercises which can be employed to introduce others to the key concepts involved.

4. Start where you can

The innovation described in Chapter 6 started with one lecturer introducing a short break into the middle of a lecture. It took a number of years and a series of small steps, evaluations and experiments to reach the model of course delivery described. Some of the case studies involved comparatively large changes and it is tempting to respond by arguing that it would obviously be impossible to introduce such a large change straight away so nothing is possible. But even these large changes were preceded by smaller experiments in previous years on other courses. It is always possible to start straight away with some level of innovation, even if it is very small. Improving teaching is an experimental process and it is possible to start tomorrow.

5. Start small

Most of the innovations described in the case studies started small. Even the complex ones, such as the problem based engineering course described in Chapter 7, started with only six students. The teaching and assessment methods involved in this course were new to the teachers involved and they needed to feel their way and learn while they developed the course. Even with plenty of development time beforehand it can be prudent to start small and give yourself some leeway to adjust. Students need to feel their way too, and may feel disoriented or even protest if the changes are too fast and too dramatic.

It is also common, in my experience, for enthusiasts to introduce too many changes at once. Not only are students asked to work in groups, for example, but they are asked to self-assess their own work, find their own reading resources and keep reflective logs, none of which they have done before. With so much changing at once it is likely that something will go wrong but you may not be able to tell exactly what. With so many variables the source of the problem may be hidden. I have seen complex innovations abandoned with no understanding of exactly what went wrong or why. Little is learnt from such experiments.

6. Don't re-invent the wheel

Most of the methods used in most of the case studies have been used extensively elsewhere in the UK, in Australia or in North America. Most are well documented. Many educational development staff know about these methods and even know others who have used them. There are excellent networks for sharing this kind of information, such as SCED (the Standing Conference on Educational Development). There is a great deal of documented experience, for example, concerning how to set up and assess group work, how to design learning packages which work and how to introduce active learning into lectures. This was not exploited to any great extent in some of the case studies and it might have helped if more had been taken from existing knowledge and experience. It is not necessary or helpful to act as if you were the first person to think of these methods. On the other hand an element of re-inventing the wheel is often necessary to customise methods so that they suit the context properly. The particular way group projects were used differed a great deal between the courses described in Chapters 7, 10 and 12 and these differences were important and necessary. Methods cannot simply be copied.

7. Change the assessment

Whatever else you choose to do to change your course, make sure you pay careful attention to the assessment system. It is no good introducing active learning into lectures and seminars if the exam questions reward regurgitation. By far the most powerful levers available to you to change the ways students approach their learning involve the assessment and to ignore these levers is a waste. Even if exam regulations constrain the scope for manoeuvre, for example by requiring three-hour unseen exams, there is usually still scope for subtle changes in the form of questions or the criteria used. In some contexts it is possible to change the assessment and leave everything else the same and achieve dramatic improvements and this can involve very little effort. For example requiring essays to be written by pairs of students and introducing a marking system based on the SOLO taxonomy could dramatically change students' focus of attention, increase interaction and make learning more active whilst halving your marking time. Once this assessment system was established you could go on to ask students to sit in their pairs in lectures to share notes and to co-operate in seminar presentations as well. Changes in assessment usually lag behind innovations in teaching but it can be very effective to lead with innovations in assessment and then exploit the teaching opportunities this throws up.

8. *Involve students*

Students can block or corrupt innovations but they can also make them work. It is partly a matter of getting students on your side, so that you are working together to make the course function and partly a matter of explaining properly why you are doing what you are doing and what are your expectations of them. It can be difficult to implement innovations if the students don't understand and don't believe in what you are trying to do. Detailed suggestions for involving students can be found in Chapter 16.

9. *Involve others*

Innovation can be a lonely and risky business. You are more likely to learn and to extend your ideas and methods if others are involved. Methods used on several modules by several lecturers have more chance of long-term survival than methods used on only one module. The most extensive innovations amongst the case studies involved initial staff training to develop a team who could all be involved. The innovations which had the widest impact were those where staff development activities followed initial experiments to spread the methods wider as quickly as possible. Those innovations where colleagues were persuaded to adopt similar methods were more likely to gain acceptance and brought into the mainstream of course design rather than left outside as oddities. Chapter 16 contains a range of exercises and materials which can be used in staff development events.

10. *Cost plans carefully*

Methods to improve quality are often assumed to cost more. None of the courses described in the case studies cost more than their conventional alternatives and several were cheaper. It is important that colleagues recognise this. As the innovations often employed a different pattern of use of staff time, for example fewer lectures but more support for groups, it is not always obvious what the real costs are. The actual costs in staff time and resources should be carefully calculated and compared with the costs of conventional alternatives. Often the running costs will be comparable but an initial investment will be necessary to introduce the change. Whether this investment will be worthwhile will depend on the perceived benefits, which leads on to the next point.

11. *Collect good evidence*

If your colleagues could be persuaded by rhetoric then they would all have changed by now. They will need good evidence if they are going to abandon methods they are familiar with to try methods they have never used before. They will need evidence both of problems with their current methods (see 2 above) and advantages which flow from alternatives. The case studies illustrate ways of collecting a laying out evidence in a form which can be convincing.

12. Document what you are doing

If you want to involve and convince others it is helpful to be able to show them what you are doing. As they probably won't come into your classrooms this usually means showing them written descriptions: the manual you have devised, your assessment criteria, the project outlines and so on. Without such documentation you will not only find it harder to explain what you are doing, you will also be less credible. It also helps to collect evidence which you can show other: examples of students' work, letters from employers and external examiners and so on. People will only believe what they can see.

13. Change as you go along

It is unlikely that you will get everything right first time. You will need to be aware of what is going well, or badly, and flexible in responding to problems. You may need to collect evaluation evidence early on rather then wait until the end of the course and you may need to change or drop elements of the course while it is in operation rather than waiting until the next time the course runs before introducing new features. Chapter 12 demonstrated how important fine tuning is in getting a course to work.

Good luck!

Chapter 16

Involving others in improving the quality of student learning

As highlighted in the previous chapter, it is hard to innovate on your own. It helps to have the students on your side and it helps to have allies who share your values and goals. This chapter contains ideas for ways to involve students, and materials to support staff development events designed to exploit this project, its rationale and outcomes.

Involving Students

It can be very effective to get students on your side in co-operatively exploring learning on your course and in trying to make innovations work. If students are more aware of what is going on and why they are more likely to respond appropriately. Students also develop and become more effective as learners the more they understand about learning. The following suggestions are offered as ways to engage students in the process of improving learning.

1. Explain what you are doing and why and that you need their active involvement if any progress is going to be made. Students usually care about the quality of their courses and are prepared to do something about quality, but they do not like being experimented on or kept in the dark about what is happening or why.

2. Ask students to complete and score the Approaches To Studying questionnaire. Make it clear that this is to help them to see how they study, and to help you to see how the whole class is studying, but that you are not interested in individual's scores. Ask them not to put their names on the questionnaires. Discuss with them their scores and what they mean. Explain what deep and surface approaches are about. This can be undertaken even with a large lecture class in about 20 minutes.

3. If students are intrigued, ask them to write down their three scores (Achieving, Reproducing and Meaning) together with their current course marks (or whatever assessment marks are most appropriate, such as their marks on their last lab report, essay or problem sheet), and collect up this data. Calculate the correlations between their scores and their marks and explain these to them at the next meeting. I have taken a microcomputer and statistics software into study skills sessions so that I can plot a regression line and students can see who gets the best marks and why. Alternatively, you can plot a graph on a transparency to display in the next lecture. Such visual representation can have a powerful impression on students, especially where it shows a clear relationship between approach and marks.

4. Ask students to interview each other for 5–10 minutes each, using the interview questions below on page 180. Ask them to try and spot where a deep or a surface approach was being used. Then have an open discussion about what emerged. This can be undertaken during a seminar or workshop session and would take about 30 minutes.

5. Explain the ways in which students' answers to questions and assignments differ in quality. The exercise shown in Table 16.1, called 'First Class Answer', is drawn from Habeshaw et al (1988). Students find it illuminating and amusing. It takes an essay question and re-writes it according to the way a student who will gain a first class degree, and upper second class degree, and so on, will interpret it.

You could do the same kind of analysis with one of your own essay questions or assignments or use this example to explain the general idea. Then ask them to take one of their next essay titles, or an exam question, and to re-write it in a similar way. Allow groups of three to work on this and display the questions they come up with. Correct misunderstandings and discuss what the exercise reveals about they way they were interpreting assessment demands and what the real demands of your course are. This can take 30–40 minutes with about 30 students.

Having introduced the general idea of qualitatively different learning outcomes, introduce students to the SOLO taxonomy and undertake Exercise 4 outlined on page 184.

6. It is also possible, once students understand what a deep approach is and what the SOLO taxonomy is about, to require them to submit a self-assessment sheet with their assignments commenting on the way they approached the assignment and on the quality of their essay, report or whatever. The pro-forma in Table 16.2 is offered as an example. It should be filled in and attached to students' assignment at the time of submission. It can be made a course requirement so that the assignment is considered incomplete without it. If students have to fill in such a sheet they will be likely to think about their approach and the quality of their work rather more.

First Class Answer

Original Question:

'Compare and contrast the effects of blindness and deafness on language development.'

First class answer:

'Identify the consequences of blindness and deafness for language development. Compare and contrast these consequences, drawing conclusions about the nature of language development and commenting on the adequacy of theories of language development.'

Upper second class answer:

'Identify the consequences of blindness and deafness for language development. Compare and contrast these consequences.'

Lower second class answer:

'List some of the features of blindness and deafness. List some consequences for language development.'

Third class answer:

'Write down anything you can think of about blindness, deafness, child development and language development in the order in which you think of things. Draw no justified conclusions.'

Table 16.1: Exercise: First Class Answer

Self-Assessment Sheet

Course ....

Name ....

Assignment ....

To what extent did you take a surface or a deep approach to this assignment? Explain your answer with descriptions of the study activities involved.

What SOLO level is your assignment at? (Circle one)

(a) PRESTRUCTURAL

(b) UNISTRUCTURAL

(c) MULTISTRUCTURAL

(d) RELATIONAL

(e) EXTENDED ABSTRACT

Justify your judgment with reference to features of your assignment.

To improve the quality of the way you went about this assignment, and to improve the assignment itself, what else might you have done?

Table 16.2: An example of a self-assessment sheet

You could also give students feedback on their work in terms of the SOLO taxonomy.

Apart from 'learning to learn' exercises of this kind which orient students to a deep approach and towards higher levels in the SOLO taxonomy, you can engage students in introducing innovations. If you explain what you are intending to do, and why, they are often perfectly capable of giving you sensible advice about how to make it work. You can also hold brief review meetings to discuss how your innovation is going, what problems there are, and what might be done to improve things. In very large classes you can set up a small feedback group, perhaps made up of representatives of seminar groups, to have coffee with once a fortnight to chat about how it is all going. The goal here is to get students working co-operatively with you to make your course a success rather than feeling they are being manipulated or experimented with. If you make decisions about how things should work, explain your decisions. If it is practical, involve students in the decision-making.

Staff development exercises and materials

The following exercises and supporting materials have been piloted in staff development workshops run at a range of institutions in the UK and also in Australia and New Zealand. They are offered as short exercises which could be introduced into course team meetings or short lunchtime seminars, or alternatively combined into a one-day event. The Oxford Centre for Staff Development has trained consultants to be able to run workshops using these materials but they are simple enough to use without assistance.

1. Preparation

It helps any staff development session if participants have done some preparation in advance. The following forms of preparation involve participants in thinking about, and doing small-scale research about, their own course.

1.1 Review of successes and blocks.

Write brief notes about one thing you have done to improve the quality of student learning in courses you teach on. What was its most important feature and why did it work?

Write brief notes on two blocks to improving student learning, one which is a feature of the course and one which is a feature of the way students study on the course.

Talk this through with a colleague or with a student if possible.

Bring your notes to the session.

1.2 Questionnaire

Administer the Approaches to Studying questionnaire to at least a sample of students on your own course. Get the students to collate their scores to save you the trouble. Before you calculate the means, try and predict what they will be in relation to the national norms. Calculate means and compare them with national norms. Try and make sense of the scores: what do they mean and why are they similar or different from national norms? Bring the results to the session.

1.3 Interview

Interview three or four students about their approaches to studying on your course (or ask a colleague or someone from your educational development unit to interview for you). Tape record and transcribe the interviews.

Ask the following questions:

- 'Tell me about what you are doing and what you are thinking about when you are taking notes/in a lecture/in a seminar/in the lab/reading a book/writing an essay etc.' Prompt with specific occasions rather than getting a general description, and follow up with more detailed questions until you feel you understand exactly what they are doing.

- 'Do you always study like that? If not can you describe how else you study?'

- 'Why do you study like that? What is it about this course that makes you study like that?'

- 'When you use the word learning, what do you mean?'

- 'What do you think gets the marks on this course?'

Read through the transcripts picking out sections which seem particularly interesting or important. Bring the transcripts to the session.

2. Exercise: Successes and blocks

Introduce those present to each other in the following way:

> 'Please say who you are and what you teach. In addition, please identify one one thing you have done to improve the quality of student learning in courses you teach on, and a block to improving student learning: either a block which is a feature of the course or one which is a feature of the way students study on the course.'

If participants have undertaken preparation (see above) use their notes and allow much more time for this initial sharing of successes and blocks.

Time: 1 - 2 minutes per participant

3. Exercise: Deep and surface approaches to learning

Stage 1

Explain what 'deep' and 'surface' approaches to learning are about, using the following definitions:

Deep Students focus their attention on the overall meaning or message in a lecture, text or situation. They attempt to relate ideas together and construct their own meaning, possibly in relation to their own experience.

Surface Students focus their attention on the details and information in a lecture or text. They are trying to memorise these individual details in the form they appear in the lecture or text or to list the features of the situation.

Stage 2

Ask participants to categorise the following four extracts from interviews with students:

A) 'I don't like having to take notes in lectures. I would prefer to concentrate on understanding. I like to be able to listen so I can understand what the problem is.' (Law)

B) 'I learn Law by cases: listing cases and listing principles. I have a good short term memory and I can memorise enough to get through exams.' (Law)

C) 'I read it, I read it very slowly, trying to concentrate on what it means, what the actual passage means. Obviously I've read the quotes a few times and I've got it in my mind, what they mean. I really try to read it slowly. There is a lot of meaning behind it. You have to really kind of get into it and take every passage, every sentence, and try to really think 'Well what does this mean?' You mustn't regurgitate what David is saying because that's not the idea of the exercise, so I suppose it's really original ideas in this one, kind of getting it all together.'
(Geography)

D) 'When you use the word learning in relation to this course, what do you mean?'
'Getting enough facts so that you can write something relevant in the exam. You've got enough information so you can write an essay on it. What I normally do is learn certain headings. I'll write a question down, about four, five different headings, which in an exam I can go: 'Introduction' and I'll look at the next heading and I know what I've got to write about without really thinking about it really. I know the facts about it. I go to the next heading and regurgitate.'
(Computing)

Participants should do this categorisation on their own, then share in pairs or threes before opening out to a discussion of what the terms deep and surface mean. Ask participants to generate statements illustrating a surface approach, and a deep approach, to their own course. If participants have prepared by interviewing students, this is the time to have a look at their transcripts and attempt to identify examples of deep and surface approaches.

Stage 3

Ask participants to complete the Approaches to Studying questionnaire. They should be asked to imagine that they are a mediocre student on their own course. If they can't do this then they should think back to a time when they were themselves a student on a course where they were required to remember a lot of information (e.g. 'O' level Latin or a first year Anatomy class) and complete the questionnaire with that course in mind.

Stage 4

Participants should be asked to score their questionnaires and to compare and discuss these scores with two other people. If participants have prepared by administering the questionnaire to any of their own students, this is the time to bring this data in and to discuss it.

Stage 5

Have an open discussion about what 'deep' and 'surface' mean in the context of participants' own courses.

Time: 60 minutes.

4. Exercise: The SOLO taxonomy

Stage 1

Explain the SOLO taxonomy using the following definitions:

The SOLO (Structures Of Learning Outcomes) Taxonomy

The taxonomy involves five levels and these levels are defined below:

(a) PRESTRUCTURAL Ignorance. No correct elements are present.

(b) UNISTRUCTURAL One correct and relevant element is present.

(c) MULTISTRUCTURAL Several relevant elements are present but are independent of each other, often in a list form.

(d) RELATIONAL These relevant elements are integrated into a structure. Students produce an argument rather than a list.

(e) EXTENDED ABSTRACT As relational, but the whole is generalised to a related domain of knowledge. This would be evident in a fist class answer where a student realised that behind a question were related questions which drew on other related issues and knowledge.

Introduce the general idea of different qualities of learning outcome using the 'First Class Answer' material above (Table 16.1) if appropriate.

Stage 2

Ask participants to categorise the following students' statements about their learning:

Examples of Learning Outcomes

Physiotherapy students talking about their work with a patient:

A) 'First I did a routine... then I did a bit of... and then I told him what he should do every morning and evening and to come and see me again in a month.'

SOLO level ....

B) 'It was a classic case of... From a purely medical point of view I'd have gone ahead with a normal treatment plan but talking with him about his social context it was clear this wouldn't have been very likely to work. So I devised a care plan with him that took advantage of the little home help he gets and accepts that he's unlikely to be able to manage a lot on his own.'

SOLO level ....

Art and Design students writing about their work experience:

C) 'Tuesday 15th. Because the people who use this stuff aren't very numerate I'm going to have to find a way to display the ideas in pictures rather than in numbers or even in graphs, so I think I'll look up examples of pictograms to get some ideas.'

SOLO level ....

D) 'In the middle of a conference with a client today I realised that what they were arguing about was exactly what Barry told us about. If you look at it from a ..... point of view then you'd decide to ...... whereas if you looked at it from a ..... then you'd go about it completely differently. You could even see it from a ... point of view though that would have led to some very funny designs in this case. I hadn't realised the practical implications of those different perspectives before.'

SOLO level ....

Get participants to classify these four examples on their own and then discuss them in groups of three or four.

Stage 3

Have an open discussion of what the SOLO categories mean and how they might apply to participants' own contexts.

Stage 4

As participants to write down examples of things their own students might say (in essays, reports or in discussions) which would reveal levels 3, 4 and 5 in relation to subject matter they have been taught. Leave them for at least five minutes for this task—it is difficult.

Then go round the group, each person in turn reading two things they have written, in order to contrast different levels of learning outcome.

Time: 45 minutes

5. Exercise: Course features which foster a surface approach

Stage 1

Explain the impact of a surface approach on the quality of student learning, using evidence and examples from Chapter 1. Invite participants to suggest what are the consequences of students taking an extreme surface approach in their own courses.

Stage 2

Explain the features of courses which evidence suggests are likely to foster a surface approach (listed below, and elaborated in Chapter 1). Ask them to use the form below to note down possible features of their own course which might accidentally induce a surface approach.

Stage 3

Ask participants to talk through their notes in groups of three or four, highlighting the greatest danger areas.

Stage 4

In the whole group, ask each participant to describe the most worrying potential cause of a surface approach on their own course, and one step which suggests itself for reducing the extent to which a surface approach might be fostered.

Time: 30 minutes

Course features which can foster a surface approach:

Heavy workload

Excessive course material

Lack of opportunity to study subjects in depth

Lack of choice over subjects

Lack of choice over methods of study

Anxiety provoking assessment system

Assessment which tolerates regurgitation

6. Exercise: Course features which foster a deep approach

Stage 1

Ask participants to read the following summary of features which foster a deep approach.

(a) Motivational context

Deep learning is more likely when students' motivation is intrinsic and when the student experiences a need to know something. Adults learn best what they need to learn in order to carry out tasks which matter to them. Students are likely to need to be involved in selecting what is to be learnt and in planning how the learning should take place if they are to experience 'ownership' of it. The motivational context is established by the emotional climate of the learning.

(b) Learner activity

Students need to be active rather than passive. Deep learning is associated with doing. If the learner is actively involved, then more connections will be made both with past learning and between new concepts. Doing is not sufficient for learning, however. Learning activity must be planned, reflected upon and processed, and related to abstract conceptions.

(c) Interaction with others

It is often easier to negotiate meaning and to manipulate ideas with others than alone. The importance of discussion for learning is not a new idea, though there is precious little discussion in much of higher education. Interaction can take many forms other than conventional tutorials and seminars, and autonomous student groups and peer tutoring can be very effective.

(d) A well structured knowledge base

Without existing concepts it is impossible to make sense of new concepts. It is vital that students' existing knowledge and experience are brought to bear in learning. The subject matter being learnt must also be well structured and integrated. The structure of knowledge is more visible to and and more useful to students where it is clearly displayed, where content is taught in integrated wholes rather than in small separate pieces, and where knowledge is required to be related to other knowledge rather than learned in isolation.

Stage 2

Ask participants to discuss, in small groups of three or four, which of these four features is evident, and in what ways and to what extent, in their own courses. Which area(s) are they possibly weak in?

Stage 3

In the whole group, ask each participant in turn to identify one area which they think they should focus on if they were to attempt to foster a deep approach to a greater extent.

Time: 30 minutes

7. Exercise: Improving student learning case studies

Stage 1

Ask participants to select one case study from this book to explore. They should make notes under the following headings so that they could explain their case study to another person:

- What is the course and what is it about?
- What was the course like before the innovation was introduced, or what would have been the conventional way of teaching it?
- What student learning problems were associated with this context? What was the innovation trying to achieve?
- What did the innovation consist of? What key features which foster a deep approach did it embody?
- What impact did the innovation have on students' approach?
- What impact did the innovation have on students' learning outcomes?
- If the impact was not as great as was intended, why not?
- What implications are there for your own course in terms of:
  - diagnosis of problems of student learning
  - using elements from the innovation
  - studying the quality of your students' learning.

Stage 2

Ask participants to find two other people who have read a different case study, and take it in turns to explain the case study they have read to each other.

Stage 3

Have an open discussion of the nature of the case studies and the implications for participants' own courses.

Time: 60 minutes

8. Exercise: Planning to improve the quality of student learning

Stage 1

Ask participants to undertake a speculative design task in which they plan an innovation in their source with the specific intention of reducing the extent of a surface approach, increase the extent of a deep approach and increasing the proportion of students' assignments at levels 4 and 5 in the SOLO taxonomy.

This design Stage takes at least 45 minutes. It is usually helpful for participants to spend at least some of this time alone. Large group discussions don't make much progress on detailed planning. Even in pairs participants may have to be disciplined in taking turns on each other's course design or they may fall into general discussion and make little progress.

Stage 2

Ask participants to display their plans on a poster under the following headings:

Poster

Course title:

Learning problem(s) addressed:

Outline of innovation:

Key features of innovation which are designed to effect students' approach:

How assessment is designed to support the innovation:

How will I know if I have succeeded?

Stage 3

Tour and discussion of posters. With a small group it may be possible to spend time on each poster in turn. With a larger group it may be necessary to have an unstructured 'tour' or to focus on two or three promising posters.

Stage 4

Action planning. Ask participants to complete the following action planning sheet on their own for 10–15 minutes. Then finish with a 'round' in which each participant in turn identifies one action he or she can take to improve the quality of student learning in their own course.

Action Planning for Improving Student Learning

What do I want to introduce, to improve the quality of student learning, in the long term?

What could stop me?

Who do I have as allies?

How could I overcome the blocks?

What can I do to set this plan in action?

What can I introduce, to improve the quality of student learning, in the short term, and which is small in scale and requires no approval or funding?

What can I do to set this plan in action?

Time: 90–120 minutes

All the material in this chapter may be copied for the purpose of staff development events or exercises with students.

References

Biggs, J.B. (1989a) Approaches to the enhancement of tertiary teaching. *Higher Education Research and Development.* 8, 7-25.

Biggs, J.B. (1989b) Does learning about learning help teachers with teaching? Psychology and the tertiary teacher. Supplement to *The Gazette* Vol. 26, No.1. University of Hong Kong.

Biggs, J.B. (1990) *Teaching Design for Learning.* Keynote paper. Brisbane: Higher Education Research and Development Society of Australasia.

Boud, D. and Felletti, G. (1991) *The Challenge of Problem Based Learning.* London: Croom Helm.

Boud, D., Keogh, R. and Walker, D. (eds.) (1985) *Reflection: Turning Experience into Learning.* London: Kogan Page.

Brophy, J. (1986) *On Motivating Students.* Occasional Paper No.101. Institute for Research on Teaching. Michigan State University.

Cohen, G., Stanhope, N. and Conway, M. (1992) How long does education last? *The Psychologist.* Vol.5 No. 2.

Crooks, T.J. (1988) The impact of classroom evaluation practices on students. *Review of Educational Research.* 58, 438-481.

Dahlgren, L-O. (1984) *Outcomes of Learning* In F.Marton, D.Hounsell and N.J.Entwist (eds.) The Experience of Learning. Edinburgh: Scottish Academic Press.

Entwistle, N. (1981) *Styles of Teaching and Learning.* Chichester: Wiley.

Entwistle, N.J. and Ramsden, P. (1983) *Understanding Student Learning.* London: Croom Helm.

Entwistle, N. and Tait, H. (1990) Approaches to learning, evaluations of teaching, and preferences for contrasting academic environments. *Higher Education.* 19, 169-194.

Gibbs, G. (1981) *Teaching Students To Learn.* Milton Keynes: Open University Press.

Gibbs, G. (1988) *Learning by Doing.* London: Further Education Unit.

Gibbs, G., Lockwood, F., Morgan, A. and Taylor, E. (1982) *Student Learning and Course Design 1: In-text Teaching Devices in Open University Texts.* Study Methods Group Report No. 12. Open University.

Gibbs, G., Morgan, A. and Taylor, E. (1984) *The World of the Learner* In F.Marton, D.Hounsell and N.J.Entwistle (eds.) The Experience of Learning. Edinburgh: Scottish Academic Press.

Habeshaw, T., Habeshaw, S. and Gibbs, G. (1989) *53 Interesting Ways Of Helping Your Students To Study.* Bristol: Technical and Educational Services.

H.M.I. (1989) *The English Polytechnics.* London: HMSO.

Knowles, M. (1986) *Using Learning Contracts.* London: Jossey-Bass.

Laurillard, D. (1979) The process of student learning. *Higher Education.* 8, 395-409.

Marton F. and Saljo, R. (1976) On qualitative differences in learning - I: outcome and process. *British Journal of Educational Psychology.* 46, 4-11.

Marton F. and Saljo. R. (1984) *Approaches to Learning.* In F.Marton, D.Hounsell and N.J.Entwistle (eds.) The Experience of Learning. Edinburgh: Scottish Academic Press.

Marton, F. and Wenestam, C.G. (1978) *Qualitative differences in the understanding and retention of the main points in some texts based on the principle-example structure.* In M.M. Gruneberg, P.E. Morris and R.N. Sykes (eds.) Practical Aspects of Memory. London: Academic Press.

Newble, D. and Clarke, R.M. (1986) The approaches to learning of students in a traditional and in an innovative problem-based medical school. *Medical Education.* 20, 267-273.

Percy, K. and Ramsden, P. (1980) *Independent Study.* Research into Higher Educstion Monographs. Guildford: Society for Research into Higher Education.

Perry, W.G. (1970) *Forms of Intellectual and Ethical Development in the College Years: A Scheme.* New York: Holt, Rinehart and Winston.

Ramsden, P. (1983) Institutional variations in British students approaches to learning and experiences of teaching. *Higher Education.* 12. 691-705.

Ramsden, P. (1984) *The Context of Learning.* In F.Marton, D.Hounsell and N.J.Entwist (eds.) The Experience of Learning. Edinburgh: Scottish Academic Press.

Ramsden, P. (1987) Improving teaching and learning in higher education: the case for a relational perspective. *Studies in Higher Education.* 12, 275-286.

Ramsden, P. (1988) *Studying Learning: Improving Teaching* In P. Ramsden, (ed.) Improving Learning: New Perspectives. London: Kogan Page.

Ramsden, P. (1991) A performance indicator of teaching quality in higher education: The Course Experience Questionnaire. *Studies in Higher Education.* 16, 129-150.

Ramsden, P., Beswick, D. and Bowden, J. (1986) Effects of learning skills interventions on first year university students learning. *Human Learning.* 5, 151-164.

Richardson, J.T.E. Reliability and replicability of the Approaches to Studying questionnaire. *Studies in Higher Education.* 15, 2, 155-168.

Rogers, C. (1969) *Freedom to Learn.* Ohio: Merrill.

Svensson, L. (1977) On qualitative differences in learning: III. Study skill and learning. *British Journal of Educational Psychology.* 47, 233-243.

Tobin, K. and Fraser, B.J. (1988) Investigations of exemplary practice in high school science and mathematics. *Australian Journal of Education* 32, 75-94.

Van Rossum, E.J. and Schenk, S.M. (1984) The relationship between learning conception, study strategy and learning outcome. *British Journal of Educational Psychology.* 54, 73-83.

Van Rossum, E.J. and Taylor, I.P. (1987) *The relationship between conception of learning and good teaching: A scheme for cognitive development.* Paper presented to the American Educational Research Association Annual Meeting: Washington.

Appendix A

The Approaches to Studying questionnaire

A short version of the Approaches to Studying questionnaire was used to monitor changes in the quality of student learning in the case studies. The Approaches to Studying questionnaire was developed at Lancaster University in the late 1970's out of extensive research into how students in higher education went about studying on their courses (see Entwistle and Ramsden, 1983). It is not a course evaluation questionnaire in the conventional sense in that it does not enquire about students' satisfaction with their courses or with their teachers. Instead it focuses on a number of qualities of what students do when they are studying. Originally the questionnaire contained 120 items concerned with students' motivation, their learning style, and the extent to which students were taking a deep and a surface approach. The questionnaire was developed, and shortened to 64 items, through several stages of improvement, interviewing in a number of institutions, incorporation of research involving the development of a similar questionnaire in Australia, and through statistical analysis. It became clear that there were three main groupings of questions. How students answered these groups of questions produced scores on three scales. These were concerned with:

A) **Strategic orientation** made up of:
Extrinsic motivation—seeing qualifications as the main source of motivation for learning.
Strategic approach—actively seeking information about assessment requirements.
Achievement orientation - being competitive and self-confident, driven by a hope for success.

B) **Reproducing orientation** made up of:
Surface approach—relying on rote learning

Syllabus-boundness—restricting learning to the defined syllabus and specified tasks.

Fear of failure—lacking self confidence and being anxiously aware of assessment requirements.

Improvidence—not looking for relationships between ideas, and being fact-bound.

C) **Meaning orientation** made up of:

Deep approach—looking for meaning in studying and interact actively with what is being learnt, linking studying with real life.

Use of evidence—students who examine evidence critically and use it cautiously.

Relating ideas—actively relating new ideas to previous knowledge.

Intrinsic motivation—being interested in learning for its own sake.

This questionnaire has been used very extensively in surveys of differences between academic departments, in surveys of the effects of students' approach on their performance, and in surveys of the relationship between characteristics of academic departments and the ways students study. A shortened 18 item version has been used at Oxford Polytechnic since 1984 for quick and convenient use in course evaluation. It was drawn from a slightly longer version, which incorporates the same scales, in Entwistle (1981). Following the questionnaire is a score sheet to enable students to interpret the results of the questionnaire.

There are several problems with this questionnaire. It assumes a relatively conventional taught course and may be of limited use in some contexts. It was not initially used in the case study in Chapter 8 concerning a graphic design course because the ways creative subjects are studied are not well reflected in the questionnaire items. It may also be dificult to distinguish between different course elements stduents are taking in parallel. Some of the items assume a coherent and uniform course rather than one made up of separate modules or elements which might make different demands. It is important to instruct students to bear in mind the specific course element being studied when they complete the questionnaire. There are also some doubts about the reliability of the three scales with shortened versions of the questionnaire. Studies have cast doubts, in particular, on the 'Achieving' scale. An alternative 30-item version of the questionnaire which includes only the 'Reproducing' and 'Meaning Scales', and which has been demonstrated to be satisfactorily reliable, is recommended in preference to the short version reproduced here for research purposes (see Richardson, 1990).

Approaches To Studying Questionnaire

Please answer every item quickly by giving your immediate response. Circle the appropriate code number to show your general approach to studying.

4 means definitely agree

3 means agree with reservations

2 is only to be used if the item doesn't apply to you, or if you find it impossible to give a definite answer.

1 means disagree with reservations

0 means definitely disagree

1. I find it easy to organise my study time effectively.   4 3 2 1 0 (A)
2. I like to be told precisely what to do in essays or other   4 3 2 1 0 (B)
set work.
3. It's important to me to do really well in the courses here.   4 3 2 1 0 (A)
4. I usually set out to understand thoroughly the meaning of   4 3 2 1 0 (C)
what I am asked to read.
5. When I'm reading I try to memorise important facts which   4 3 2 1 0 (B)
may come in useful later.
6. When I'm doing a piece of work, I try to bear in mind exactly 4 3 2 1 0 (A)
what that particular lecturer seems to want.
7. My main reason for being here is so that I can learn more   4 3 2 1 0 (C)
about the subjects which really interest me.
8. I suppose I'm more interested in the qualifications I'll get than 4 3 2 1 0 (B)
in the courses I'm taking.
9. I'm usually prompt in starting work in the evenings.   4 3 2 1 0 (A)
10. I generally put a lot of effort into trying to understand things 4 3 2 1 0 (C)
which initially seem difficult.
11. Often I find I have to read things without having a chance to   4 3 2 1 0 (B)
really understand them.
12. If conditions aren't right for me to study, I generally manage   4 3 2 1 0 (A)
to do something to change them.
13. I often find myself questioning things that I hear in lessons or 4 3 2 1 0 (C)
read in books.
14. I tend to read very little beyond what's required for completing 4 3 2 1 0 (B)
assignments.
15. It is important to me to do things better than my friends, if I   4 3 2 1 0 (A)
possibly can.
16. I spend a good deal of my spare time in finding out more   4 3 2 1 0 (C)
about interesting topics which have been discussed in class.
17. I find academic topics so interesting, I should like to continue 4 3 2 1 0 (C)
with them after I finish this course.
18. I find I have to concentrate on memorising a good deal of   4 3 2 1 0 (B)
what we have to learn.

This questionnaire and the three scales it contains is based on the short version of the Approaches to Studying questionnaire in Entwistle (1981) and is reproduced here with the permission of Wiley.

Approaches To Studying Questionnaire Score Sheet

Score your questionnaire by writing down the numbers circled for questions marked A, B or C. There should be six numbers for each. Then add up the totals for the columns A, B, and C.

A	B	C
Totals		

'A' scale score

This is a score out of 24 on 'Achieving orientation'. This indicates competitiveness, well organised study methods, and hope for success. Students who score high on this scale are oriented towards doing well, whatever this involves. They tend to do well.

'B' scale score

This is a score out of 24 on 'Reproducing orientation'. This indicates a surface approach to learning. Students who score high on this scale attempt to memorise subject matter and are not interested in studying a subject for its own sake but only out of a concern to pass or gain qualifications. They keep narrowly to the syllabus as laid down in course descriptions and do not follow up interests of their own (if they have any). Despite their concern to pass they tend to do badly.

'C' scale score

This is a score out of 24 on 'Meaning orientation'. This indicates a deep approach to learning: the intention to make sense of the subject, an interest in the subject itself, and a desire to learn. Students who score high on this scale follow up their own interests even if these are outside those parts of the course which are assessed. They tend to do well. Norms are available from large-scale national studies (Entwistle and Ramsden, 1983) so you can compare your scores with national averages.

Scale	Arts	Social Science	Science	Overall	Standard deviation
(A) Achieving	12.50	12.73	13.08	12.82	4.26
(B) Reproducing	11.98	13.65	14.26	13.51	4.40
(C) Meaning	15.17	14.21	13.93	14.31	4.51